Banking in Europe After 1992

Banking in Europe After 1992

CARLOS JAVIER MOREIRO GONZALEZ

Dartmouth
Aldershot • Brookfield USA • Hong Kong • Singapore • Sydney

Published by
Dartmouth Publishing Company Limited
Gower House
Croft Road
Aldershot
Hants GU11 3HR
England

Dartmouth Publishing Company
Old Post Road
Brookfield
Vermont 05036
USA

Library of Congress Cataloging-in-Publication Data
Moreiro Gonzalez, Carlos Javier
Banking in Europe after 1992 / Carlos Javier Moreiro Gonzalez.
p. cm.
Includes bibliographical references.
ISBN 1-85521-362-1 : $69.95 (approx.)
1. Banks and banking–European Economic Community countries.
2. Banking law–European Economic Community countries. 3. Financial services industry–European Economic Community countries.
4. Financial institutions–Law and legislation–European Economic Community countries. 5. Europe 1992. I. Title.
HG2980.5.A6M65 1993
332.1'094–dc20 93–18024
CIP

ISBN 1 85521 362 1

Printed in Great Britain at the University Press, Cambridge

To my family, and also to all those friends and professors who gave me their love and support during the many difficult moments arising during the completion of this work.

Contents

Foreword

Emile Noël

This work by Carlos Moreiro is a stimulating contribution to our knowledge both of the legal system of the European Community and also to the Community legislative process.

The harmonization of laws governing banks and other credit institutions is a precondition for the achievement of the freedom to provide financial services and the freedom of establishment of credit institutions and their subsidiaries. In turn, the latter is essential to the completion of the internal market in financial services. Hence the importance and the subtlety of Community legislation in this matter, not only from the legal and economic standpoints but also in relation to the security of financial transactions. The originality of this work by Carlos Moreiro lies in the fact that the book takes account of all these aspects and provides a convincing synthesis of their interrelationship.

Carlos Moreiro addresses these questions from a legal point of view but also with the perspective of a political scientist. In this respect, his book is an excellent illustration of the contextual approach to law, which is characteristic of the research undertaken at the European University Institute. At the same time, it provides a lucid and penetrating critical evaluation of the way in which the interests in question are presented and defended, including those of the banking sector, administrative authorities and consumers. Many will benefit from this study, in particular those in the Commission, the European Parliament and the Council who are involved in the Community legislative process.

Carlos Moreiro was among the first Spanish researchers to be admitted to the European University Institute. He was awarded his doctorate following a brilliant oral examination of his thesis, on which this book is partly based. The publication of this work testifies to the high quality of the contribution which researchers from Spain, now more and more numerous, are making to the European University Institute. I extend to Carlos Moreiro my most sincere congratulations.

Emile Noël
President
European University Institute
Florence

Preface

The future of the European Community is being shaped in the current debates concerning the Maastricht Treaty. From detailed accounts of these debates it is often difficult to discern even the outlines of the institutional and political architecture of Western Europe of the twenty-first century. If one takes a broader perspective, however, it is clear that, so far, two important points have emerged. On the one hand, the general implications of Community law and policy concern everyone in Europe, although at one time it may have been thought that they were of interest only to specialists. On the other hand, the major choices of Community policy must involve political participation, instead of relying only on administrative negotiation and judicial decisions. Strengthened by these lessons, the Community and its Member States may now be able better to confront the challenges of the future.

What roles can the academic lawyer and academic legal research play in this process? Lawyers in the academy, government and private practice have often been viewed as technicians. Their tasks are frequently described as being to give an exposition of legal rules and put them in apparently systematic form, translate policy decisions into arcane legal language, and advise clients and argue court cases concerning detailed points of law. This model of the lawyer's role remains prominent even in the field of Community law. Although the field is still young, it is nevertheless surprising that such a narrow role should be prescribed as the ideal since the constitutional and administrative law of the Community, not to mention its economic and social law, are deeply imprinted with economic and political objectives. A thorough knowledge of positive law in the field of Community law is, of course, essential. But surely Community law provides a singularly appropriate field for the study of law in context – an approach which places the law in the midst of the society in which it develops and operates. The elaboration of such a method for understanding Community law is doubtless the task principally of academic lawyers, except in so far as lawyers outside the academy observe and record their practical, craft knowledge. Its fruits, however, cannot fail to interest their legal colleagues elsewhere, as well as all those outside the field of Community law who are concerned with the future of Europe. They illuminate the relationship between law and society – and the role of law in society – in the Community of the present and of the future.

The study of Community law in its political, economic and social context is now being undertaken by scholars in many countries. A pioneer in this respect has been the Department of Law at the European University Institute in Florence. The EUI, including its Law Department, is devoted primarily to the training of postgraduate students and to carrying out research. Among institutions of higher education, it thus occupies a privileged position and, one may suggest, bears correspondingly greater responsibilities. The research on Community law, and on law generally, carried out at the EUI testifies to the fact that law in context is not a unified approach, nor, at least for the time being, should it be. It takes many methodological forms and assumes many theoretical guises, each of which contributes potentially to the elaboration of an intellectually broader, more theoretically sensitive understanding of Community law.

At first glance the harmonization of banking law in the Community may appear to be an unexpected, if not intractable, subject for research from a contextual standpoint. Not only is the subject highly technical and information regarding its moving forces often difficult to obtain, but it also involves the Community's major trading partners – in particular the USA – thus demanding a knowledge which is not always easy to acquire. Theories of economic integration could of course be brought to bear on this topic, just as political theories of institutional structures or of interests, for example, might seem to lend themselves naturally to a study of Community constitutional and administrative law. But a broader view of the harmonization of banking law, combining both political and economic perspectives with that of comparative national and Community law, is difficult to achieve. Yet it is precisely the conjunction of these perspectives which is among the principal merits of this study by Carlos Moreiro.

As one who has followed the development of this work since its inception at the EUI, I can attest to the fact that Carlos Moreiro writes with both deep passion and broad knowledge of his subject. He undertakes three difficult tasks. First, he aims to analyse the ways in which the process of the harmonization of banking laws within the Community has unfolded. Second, he seeks to present, from the standpoint of several disciplines, the forces underlying this process. Third, he tries to identify some of the principal issues which the process raises, not only for specialists in Community law but also for consumers and citizens. Each of these tasks is carried out with a commitment to legal scholarship and to political democracy. Quite apart from the considerable intrinsic interest of this work, such a combination invests this study with a greater importance than might be expected of a book about law.

It is a truism to say that no work of scholarship is ever complete. This applies with special force perhaps to studies of law in context. Anyone who has tried to immerse himself or herself in another discipline in order to illuminate the development and operation of law will recall the constant struggle to learn 'just a little more' of the other social sciences, the better to elaborate a theory of law in society or law and society, while at the same time remaining anchored in the discipline of law and contributing to it. This tension between disciplines can be productive, but it increases considerably the difficulty of arriving at an intellectually convincing synthesis. This book shows, however, that such a synthesis is possible. It exemplifies the way in which perspectives from different disciplines may be combined in the study of Community law in context. More broadly, and more importantly, it demonstrates how the academic lawyer specializing in Community law may contribute to the continuing debate concerning the shaping of Europe.

Francis Snyder
Florence

List of Abbreviations

AEB	Asociacioń Española de Banca (Spanish Bankers Association)
BEUC	Bureau Europeene des Unions de Consommateurs
BIS	Bank for International Settlements
BFEC	Banking Federation of the European Community
COREPER	Committee of Permanent Representatives
DIDMCA	Depositary Institutions Deregulation and Monetary Control Act
EC	European Community
Ecofin	Council of Finance Ministers
Ecosoc	Economic and Social Committee
EEC	European Economic Community
EFTPOS	Electronic Fund Transfers Personal Offering Services
EIB	European Investment Bank
EP	European Parliament
ESCB	European System of Central Banks
EUI	European University Institute (Florence)
FDIC	Federal Deposit Insurance Corporation
FED	Federal Reserve (US)
GARN	St Germain Depositary Institutions Act
SEA	Single European Act
SEC (ESC)	Social and Economic Committee

Introduction

This book takes an interdisciplinary approach to the EEC banking harmonization process. The methodology employed consists in focusing the subject from the legal, economic and political science perspectives. Therefore, the underlying purpose of the book is to study the legal outcomes within their context.

Part I takes a legal approach to the second Banking Directive as the cornerstone of the EEC banking harmonization process. The detailed analysis of this Directive from an EEC legal perspective is a prerequisite for the understanding of how Community financial policy is being shaped.

Part II takes a political-scientific approach to the role of interests within the EC decision-making process. More specifically, it is an attempt to show how banks can influence legislators for the achievement of their objectives.

A socioeconomic approach to credit institutions' strategies for the controlling of financial markets is the theme of Part III. Through the study of the United States' current 'deregulatory' trends, I demonstrate the interrelationship between the world financial markets. A second stage of this Part links the European context to the other representative world financial markets. In this way similar behaviours can be noted, which are to conclude that neither national governments, nor the European institutions are currently capable of regulating the financial markets without a previous 'consensus' with the financial institutions.

Part IV of the research takes a critical approach to the institutional behaviour of the Community as regards policy-making for the achievement of an integrated financial market by 1992. This analysis shows that credit institutions, whose profits are greatly affected by public policy, have an extraordinary capacity to innovate and adapt, notably as a way of lawfully avoiding the effects of 'public controls'.

PART I

A LEGAL APPROACH TO THE EC BANKING HARMONIZATION PROCESS

1 The Directive 89/646: The Second Banking Directive

Preliminary Steps to the Second Banking Directive

In this section I shall analyse the proposal of the Commission and the different amendments of the European Parliament (EP) and the Social and Economic Committee (SEC or ESC) during the first reading procedure.

Most opinions agree in recognizing that the first proposal for the Second Banking Directive[1] contained a wider range of objectives for the achievement of a 'unified banking market' in Europe, than the First Banking Directive. As Lord Cockfield remarked:

> The first banking Directive, setting out common prudential criteria for the establishment and operation of banks in Member States and its corollaries on supervision and accounting laid the foundation. The Commission's proposals for the freedom of capital movement are the walls of the internal market's financial wing. Today's proposal puts the roof on the building ....[2]

The proposal has to be seen within the legal context in which it was prepared. In this sense, I should like to mention several aspects connected to the content of the proposal.

The Second Banking Coordinating Directive was intended to follow up and supplement the first. However, it adopts a radically different approach. In the second Directive the principle of mutual recognition replaces the principle of harmonization. The legal basis for this approach is to be found in the decision of the European Court of Justice in case 120/78 *Cassis de Dijon*.[3] As stated there, when a product (in this case, the financial product) has been legally manufactured and marketed according to the provisions of one Member State, it may be freely offered for sale throughout the Community regardless of the specifications obtaining in the countries of destination.

The mutual recognition of authorization is linked to the standardization of conditions governing activity and monitoring, and also to the liberalization of capital flows. But we can distinguish between this double parallelism. Parallelism between the mutual recognition of licences for banking activities and standardization should be *strict*. The reciprocal recognition of licences will enter into force *at the same time* as the various measures standardizing conditions of access to banking activities, their implementation, monitoring and controls. With regard to the parallelism between the liberalization of banking activities and the free movement of capital the Community must make progress in both domains, but there is *no precondition*. We must not wait for the realization of banking standardization before realizing the integral free movement of capital.

With regard to Community's position in the GATT, the GATT rules currently apply to trading in goods but not in services. The gradual liberalization in this last area represented one of the fundamental aspects of the Uruguay Round. Any evolution towards liberalization within the GATT Round could change the conditions of 'reciprocity' called for by third countries in article 7 of the proposal.

The proposal's objectives can be divided into those with a socioeconomic aim and those whose aim is to achieve higher standards of harmonization.

The Commission distinguished three socioeconomic objectives in the preliminary explanations to the proposal:

(1) les opérations financières à travers les frontières seront rendues plus faciles et moins coûteures ....

(2) la concurrence renforcée entre les établissements de crédit procurera un éventail de choix plus large et une réduction du coût des services bancaires ...

(3) L'innovation des techniques financières ...'[4]

These objectives which, from an economic point of view, are in accordance with the aims of the internal market omit other desirable aims, such as the protection of social policy or consumer protection interests. If we compare these objectives with the content of the conclusions from the Cecchini Report[5] we note that they are also directed to convincing Member States of the desirability of dismantling national barriers. Perhaps the Commission tried a much more realistic approach than in previous years in order to gain competence from Member States in this field, and set aside other aims such as the promotion of the policies mentioned above.

With regard to objectives for the achievement of higher standards of harmonization, we can distinguish three fields in which the proposal makes very interesting innovations.

1 A single Community licence: This means that the approval obtained by a bank in one Member State will be accepted by all the other Member States. A consequence for the exercise of banking activities is the 'home country control' principle, which means that the supervisory authorities of the Member State granting the licence are solely responsible for the prudential control of branches established as subsidiaries in another Member State. It should be noted that, if a bank so wishes, it can choose to establish a subsidiary, rather than a branch, in another Member State. In that case, the subsidiary will have a separate legal entity, submitted to full authorization and control by the supervisory authorities of the host Member State.

The proposal adds a series of standards to the prudential rules achieved under the First Banking Directive (1977) and the Directive on Supervision on a Consolidated Basis (1983). These are:

- a minimum capital of 5 M ecus;
- information on major shareholders;
- level of involvement in non-banking activities (not beyond 50 per cent of the bank's own funds and not more than 10 per cent in one undertaking).

2 A full range of banking services: There is an extensive list in the annex to the proposal. Any activity on the list covered by the authorization granted in the home country is automatically valid in the host country, even if these activities are not open to the national banks of that country. Thus advertising, for example, will be conducted in the host country under the rules of the home country, with the only possible restriction justified on grounds of public order.

3 Reciprocity requirement for third countries: Third-country banks wishing to open subsidiaries in the Community will file the relevant application for a licence with the supervisory authority of the particular Member State in which they want to establish. But the actual granting of the licence by that supervisory authority will depend on a Community procedure which will evaluate whether banking institutions from all Member States enjoy reciprocity in the applicant's state, and what measures might be taken if this is not the case.

These objectives were criticized by the EP, the ESC and, of course, the Banking Federation of the EC. We shall now review their respective positions.

The position of the EP can be synthesized in three aspects: a broader field for the application of the Directive, a stronger control on the measures for the supervision of credit institutions; and an institutional reinforcement for the competence of the Commission in this field.[6] This position is justified for several reasons:

a the independence of its members who are, at least apparently, removed from any kind of influence by pressure from banking lobbies and nationalistic positions;
b the coherence with its position regarding the First Banking Directive's project in which the aim of gaining competence the harmonization process was the most important objective;
c The protection of citizen's interests as customers of banking activities, which is clearly manifested in the aim of creating a broader field for the application of the Directive and a stronger control on the measures for the supervision of credit institutions.

It is also to be mentioned the opinion of the SEC,[7] shares most of the views within the EP's opinion.

On the other hand, four important remarks were made by the Banking Federation on points where the European Commission's proposal lacks coherence:[8]

1 On the possibility for Member States to edict more severe norms than those contained in the draft Directive: the banks of countries which are to adopt 'stricter standards' will be in an unfavourable position vis-à-vis their competitors.
2 On the overly restrictive definition of establishments to which the Directive shall be applied, which excludes financial bodies that exclusively either only collect or grant funds: the same rules should apply to all financial bodies which call on the public.
3 On the level of participation in non-banking activities: the limits of 50 per cent (own resources) and 10 per cent (individual enterprise) are too low and do not take account of the realities existing in some Member States.
4 On the special dispositions for activities concerning the securities business (shares, bonds, and so on: the Banking Federation opposes the disposition according to which the national authorities of one Member State may demand that the bank which undertakes these activities have sufficient provisions in that Member State. This is a breach in the general principle of control of the country of origin and implies a separation (which is artificial and arbitrary) between the various activities of a bank (from the point of view of surveillance of its solvency).

It is worth noting the evolution of the Banking Federation in respect of their influence in the process of drafting the First Banking Directive. In this respect, two aspects can be remarked upon. First, those who criticize the Commission's proposals are seeking a wider margin for the activities of all European banks throughout the EC. The Banking Federation has moved from its 'protectionist and nationalistic' position of 15 years ago to a more European position. Therefore it is unsurprising that it only comments on questions related to business, and neglect the social function of banking activities. Has it also moved from its original position (mainly with regard to retail banking benefits) as a result of the Cecchini Report? Second, there is no mention of the position of article 7 which claims reciprocity in the relations with third countries.

Two factors may underly this evolution. The first is economic growth, reflecting on both macroeconomic parameters and the financial markets' microeconomic field. The second is the interrelationship of the European markets, mostly through the issue of new financial instruments and the participation of the largest credit institutions in Europe within the various European stock exchanges.[9]

The Second Proposal for a Second Banking Directive

From the three aspects that synthesized the position of the EP and the SEC in their opinions on the Commission's first proposal, only one (a stronger control on measures for the supervision of credit institutions) was retained in the second proposal.

The content of this amendment has influenced several articles. Their main features are:

- *Recital 14*: '… the mutual recognition of financial techniques in the field of mortgage credit …'
- *Article 4*: '… the supervision of major shareholders …' (This ensures that the banking supervisory authorities are bound to refuse the granting of a banking licence if they consider that shareholders or members are not suitable persons.)
- *Article 7*: '… the reciprocity provisions governing the establishments in the Community of subsidiaries of banks from non-Community countries …'

The new article makes clear that 'national treatment' must really work in practice, ensuring effective market access in the third country. There may be situations where, on the face of it, the Community institution is given the same rights of establishment as a domestic bank but is excluded from the market by other means. In these circumstances the Commission would be able to act. But any country providing genuine national treatment to Community banks would be under no threat.

Article 16(1) Second Paragraph

This provision is considered necessary in order to accommodate the problems encountered by a number of regional savings banks in Germany which are confined under the terms of their licences to operating within a limited geographical area. The derogation provided by a new amendment to the general rules of article 16(1) (the right of credit institutions to provide services on the whole territory of the Community), is proposed subject to the provisions that (a) the local banks in question remain subject to all the prudential requirements imposed by Community legislation and (b) there are no barriers to competition from banks having their head office in other Member States.

Article 19(3)

This amendment makes it clear that any duly authorized credit institution must be allowed full access to all the normal means of mass-advertising its services and products. It would remain open to Member States to regulate the form and content of advertisements and also to control such practices as 'doorstep-selling' or 'cold calling', where such regulations are justified by the general good.

List of Banking Activities

The amendments regarding some items of the list were considered necessary in order to clarify the text and to bring it more closely in line with the list of services annexed to the proposal for an Investment Services Directive – activities which are also performed with increasing frequency by banks in most of the Member States. The investment activities (trading on own account or on account of customers) are: brokerage; dealing as principal; market-making, portfolio management; arranging or offering underwriting services; professional investment advice; safekeeping and administration.

The Second Council Directive 89/646, of 15.12.1989

The Directive,[10] on which the Council reached a common position on 24 July 1989,[11] illustrates the new approach to supervisory legislation in the field of financial services.[12] This feature is recognized by many of its commentators (for example, Clarotti, Zavvos and Rosello).[13]

The four substantive titles of the Directive contain both provisions to supplement the First Directive (as regards common authorization requirements (Title II), the treatment of branches of institutions established in a third country (Title III), further provisions on the pursuit of credit activities (Title IV), and new provisions primarily designed to facilitate the free provision of banking services (Title V).

I now consider some of the recitals of the Preamble to the Directive, which, in my view, add new legal contents with respect to the First Directive.

In recital 4 the spirit of the Directive and its evolution with respect to the First Directive is synthesized in the statement that:

> ... to achieve only the essential harmonization necessary and sufficient to secure the mutual recognition of authorization and of prudential supervision systems making possible the granting of a single licence recognized throughout the Community and the application of the principle of home Member State prudential supervision ....

Recital 8 can be divided into two parts. The first is intended to avoid the 'fraud of law':

> ... the principles of mutual recognition and of home Member State control require the competent authorities of each Member State not to grant authorization or to withdraw it where factors make it quite clear that a credit institution has opted for the legal system of one Member State for the purpose of evading the stricter standards in force in another Member State in which it intends to carry on or carries on the greater part of its activities ....

The second part was the consequence of long debate and was added to the Directive only during the Council discussions which preceded the Common Position of 24 July 1989. The content reiterates the various rulings of the European Court of Justice on the legality of decisions from the Commission addressed to legal persons:

> ... a credit institution shall be deemed to be situated in the Member State in which it has its registered office; Member States must require that the head office be situated in the same Member State as the registered office ....

In recital 10 we clearly see a political compromise in order to avoid distortions on the national economies of the Member States:

> … the host Member States's competent authorities will retain responsibility for the supervision of liquidity and monetary policy ….

Recital 15 allows the host Member State to require compliance with specific provisions of its own national laws: '… compatible with Community law and intended to protect the general good …' and so on. This solution has been stated before by the European Court of Justice in several cases, as for example: *Dassonville*, (1974); *Debauve* (1980); *Sandoz* (1983); *Cinéthèque* (1985); *Gullung* (1988).[15]

In recital 16 the Directive leaves aside any possibility of establishing a solution for the problems created by each specific contract for the provisions of financial services. This is a matter of private international law, and any solution must be in coherence with the process developed by the Community for the unification of norms of private international law relating to contracts. The solution to these problems must be found under the Rome Convention of 19 June 1980.[16] It is worth noting the meaning of the expression '… carrying on activities receiving mutual recognition in the same manner as in the home Member State …' This expression was preferred by the Council to that of 'financial techniques'.[17] Two consequences from its content can be considered:

1 The expression does not hinder the right of the contracting parties to choose the law that they should like to apply to the contract. Thus, there is no compulsory requirement for the application of the law of the home Member State.
2 What the expression means is that credit institutions have the right (but not the obligation) to choose the home Member State law each time they are going to carry out activities receiving mutual recognition.

In recital 18 there is an innovation in respect of the First Banking Directive whereby Member States are no longer allowed to use the 'criterion of economic needs of the market'. On the other hand, the content of the recital provides a useful link to the liberalization of capital movements. These are the national barriers to the achievement of a 'unified financial market'. In the words of the recital:

> … in any case the measures regarding the liberalization of banking services must be in harmony with the measures liberalizing capital movements ….

> ... Member States may invoke safeguard clauses in respect of capital movements, they may suspend the provision of banking services to the extent necessary for the implementation of the above mentioned safeguard clauses ....

Recital 20 from a political compromise reached by the Council in one of its last meetings.[18] Two important consequences derive from it. First, with the words 'a flexible procedure is therefore needed to make it possible to assess reciprocity on a Community basis', the Directive is confirming and delimiting the spirit of the First Banking Directive so far as the creation of a 'European Banking Policy is concerned. Second, with the words 'the aim of this procedure is not to close the Community's financial markets but rather, as the Community intends to keep its financial markets open to the rest of the world, to improve the liberalization of the global financial markets in other third countries', the Directive is opening a road to the possible inclusion of financial services in the GATT Round negotiations.

The concept of 'credit institution' in article 1(1) (taken from article 1 of the Directive 77/780 EEC) was the object of confrontations between two schools of thought reflecting, to a great extent, national philosophies on banking supervision and regulation. One approach advocates the so-called 'narrow' or 'traditional' approach, and its adherents (the United Kingdom and the Netherlands) consider that the primary objective of prudential supervision is the protection of the public's savings. They allege that any broadening of the current Community definition would incur technical problems with regard to the supervisory standards which should be set for specific institutions. The opposing, 'broader' view propounded by Germany and France) advocates that, nowadays, the purpose of prudential supervision is not only to protect savings but also to safeguard the stability of the banking system and to ensure equivalent regulatory treatment. This stability, it is argued, could be endangered by the failure of an institution which is engaged exclusively in lending activities but which finances such lending from the interbank market.[19] The Federal Republic of Germany (as it then was) made a reservation in order to include investment societies within the concept of credit institutions.[20] The solution to this conflict between national philosophies on banking supervision could come, in the future, by way of the Commission's proposal concerning investment services on the securities market.[21]

Perhaps the crux of the argument for regulatory differences as regards specialized financial institutions lies in the belief that the free market will not serve certain segments of the populace to a degree consistent with their social welfare. Thus specialized financial institutions are necessary to allocate credit and resources into certain sectors of the economy, such as housing.[22]

It may be suggested, however, that financial transactions are governed by a complex network of processes which are not always clearly understood by the public. It would therefore be advisable to extend the definition of 'credit institution' to include undertakings which grant loans without directly drawing on public deposits or other redeemable capital. In article 1(5) the Directive uses the definition of 'competent authorities' from article 1 of Directive 83/350/EEC. This concept was also fully negotiated within the Council, however, and a useful explanation finally prepared. The latter was that:

> ... pour aller à la rencontre de la délégation du *Royaume-Uni* qui a émis une réserve liée au sort des articles 14 et 17, le Groupe s'est orienté vers la solution qui consiste à insérer au procés-verbal du Conseil la déclaration suivante ....

And in article 1, point 5:

> Le Conseil et la Commission conviennent que la définition d'autorité compétente couvre, pour les besoins de la directive, les autorités nationales habilitées en vertu de dispositions légales ou réglementaires à exercer la surveillance prudentielle des établissements de crédit en ce qui concerne les activités citées sur la liste en annexe ....[23]

In article 1(6) there is a definition, by exclusion, of 'financial institution':

a an undertaking other than a 'credit institution'
b which cannot carry on these activities: acceptance of deposits and other repayable funds from the public, credit reference service and safe custody service.

This definition constitutes an innovation with respect to the First Banking Directive. Its legal consequences are linked to the content of article 18(2) of the Second Directive. In the words of P. Clarotti:

> ... cette définition est importante pour la mise en oeuvre de la reconnaissance mutuelle en faveur de certaines entreprises qui ne répondent pas à la définition d'établissement de crédit, qui est prévue à l'article 18/2/. En effet, la Commission avait estimé, et le Conseil l'a admis, qui le système de reconnaissance mutuelle à travèrs le simple recours à la liste, aurait avantagé les banques universelles des pays ayant la réglémentation la plus laxiste par rapport aux banques des pays qui interdisent ou découragent l'exercise direct par celles-ci de certaines des activités figurant dans la liste. Pour pouvoir exercer ces activités, les banques en question sont obligées de créer des filiales specialisées ....[24]

In article 2(3) there is an exemption to the application of an article of the Directive to credit institutions which are affiliated to a central body. This implies the abrogation of the 'time limit' contained in article 4(a) of the First Banking Directive (77/780; EEC).

Article 3 is a mandatory requirement for Member States, in order to prohibit persons or undertakings that are not credit institutions from carrying on the business of taking deposits or other repayable funds from the public. However, the expression 'carrying on the business' is not equally understood by the different national legislations – For example, in the French or the Spanish text this expression is understood as a 'professional activity' ('à titre professionnel' or 'a título profesional'). Such a concept does not have a common feature within EC Law and, for this reason, the European Court of Justice in the cases *Unger* and *Levin*[25] stated that it was necessary to give a common definition to this concept. It may be suggested, however, that the expression 'activities with an economic aim' used by the European Court in the cases *Van Roosmalen* and *Dona*[26] would be more adequate for the purposes of the article. The lack of a common definition of the concept could imply differences when Member States prohibit persons or undertakings from carrying on the activities cited in the article.

Article 4(1) established an initial capital holding of 5 million ecu for credit institutions as a 'minimum' requirement for authorization from the competent authorities of Member States. This requirement is a 'complement' to article 3 of the First Banking Directive. During the discussions within the Council Denmark favoured the requirement of a higher quantity of 'initial capital' for certain credit institutions with a strong risk involved in their activities (as, for example, 'mortgage credit institutions').[27]

Article 4(2) is the result of pressure from Italy and Germany within the Council for the protection of their 'regional banks'. But the situation created by this article could provoke future distortions of competition and therefore needs the application of a complementary measure in the Directive. In my view, if, at the same time, a system were set up under which credit institutions could claim exemption from the field of application of the Second Banking Directive by providing notification (on a voluntary or compulsory basis) of their decision to waive their right to extend their operations beyond the previously established territorial borders and, notably their right to undertake cross border operations, the problems facing public regional law or local credit institutions (notably in Germany) would be solved.

The initial capital required by both articles 4(1) and 4(2) is, in my view, less important, perhaps, than other factors. There is no doubt that many small credit institutions – principally, but not exclusively, cooperatives – have been operating smoothly and successfully for many years and providing a reliable service for their customers, even though their initial capital was substantially less than the limits provided by the present Directive.

Article 5(1) obliges the shareholders of members of a credit institution to inform the competent authorities about their identities and sizes of holding before taking up business. The ownership and control of a credit institution by important shareholders is an issue of supervisory concern, particularly in a period when highly complex group structures are a widespread phenomenon. Financial markets rely primarily on the confidence of the public. The particular feature of financial services is that their value is highly dependent on the public's perception of both a specific financial institution's stability and that of the financial system as a whole. The purpose of stability is not always best served by the free play of market forces, since unlimited competition can sometimes produce instability. Thus, the risk of cross-financing and conflicts of interest are particularly evident in an environment of vast changes in the structure of financial systems. Article 5(1) enables the competent authorities to obtain the necessary information regarding the identity and the interests of shareholders directly or indirectly holding a qualified participation in the credit institution applying for a licence. With this legal requirement the Directive employs a practice of the EC Commission, each time it addressed decisions to undertakings in order to decide the compatibility of their agreements with the EEC Treaty. A good example is the series of decisions in the case, *Transocean Marine Paint Association.*[28]

Article 5(2) states that the competent authorities shall refuse authorization if they are not satisfied as to the suitability of the shareholders or members of credit institution. This statement was added in the second project of the Directive (June 1989). In my view, it is another example of an arbitrary figure within the Directive, and it permits Member States to act in their own individual interests. What is meant by 'suitability'? What legal instruments can be used in order to counter a refusal of authorization based on the need to ensure the sound and prudent management of a credit institution? Once more, political compromise has brought a solution needing a prior coordination process and involving divergences derived from differing national legislations. This has affected the uniform application of the Directive within the EC. These types of requirement have also drawn criticism from well known US Scholars. Scott[29] and Rockoff,[30], as well as Posner[31], consider that all regulatory impediments to entry, based on the 'convenience and needs' requirement should be abolished. Peltzman[32] and Lash, on the other hand,[33] take the opposite view.

Article 7 makes another innovation with respect to the First Banking Directive. The aim of 'prior consultation' required by the article is to avoid the fraud of law.[34]

Articles 8 and 9 constitute Title III of the Directive (relations with third countries). Due to their complexity and importance for the application of the Directive, we shall study them together.

The Council decided, on a proposal from the French delegation,[35] to modify the Commission's original proposal[36] into a new one, with two articles. In this way the Council wished to distinguish between the obligations of the Member States in respect to the Commission and the essential questions which could affect the Community as a whole.

With the adoption of the reciprocity clause, the Community acquires a provision which already exists in the legislation of the most liberal states (for instance, the United Kingdom and Switzerland). It gives a legal content to something that is an undeniable fact: that the European Community is one of the most liberal and open financial markets in the world. For several decades, large numbers of non-Community banks, insurance companies and investment companies have been established in almost all of the EC countries and offer a broad range of financial services. In many cases, non-Community institutions are entitled to offer a broader range of services on Community territory than in their home country. However, several questions must be resolved after the coming into force of articles 8 and 9:

1 The Community must adopt a strong position in the GATT negotiations on the liberalization of financial services, given that it is one of the most open financial markets in the world, with 320 million depositors and investors. There are still many developed and developing countries which, while benefiting from the Community's open banking market, do not themselves offer Community banks and other financial institutions equal access and operating conditions. The problem may only be solved by means of 'exemptions'. The Commission has indicated its willingness to act through 'exemptions',[37] but which developing countries are going to be exempted? What criteria are going to be used for the selection of these countries?
2 If articles 8 and 9 come into force with the other articles of the Second Banking Directive at the end of 1992, the banks of countries which apply protectionist measures and hinder the access, or operations, of Community banks will rush to become established in the Community within the transitional period.
3 While today it is theoretically possible for any non-Community bank to set up branches throughout the Member States (with permission), there is no Community provision obliging these branches to respect certain minimum rules which Community banks are themselves obliged to respect – for example, banking licences, initial capital, sufficient funds, and so on.

As regards subsidiaries, despite special authorization which is currently required by most EC Member States, problems will arise regarding other issues. For instance, in a recent parliamentary question,[38] Mr De Vries MEP stressed that, under the American Bank Holding Company Act, European bank subsidiaries are not authorized to acquire insurance companies in the USA nor to merge with them, while the US banks are not under this restriction.

4 Among other preconditions, the authorities of the Member States should require the parent companies of these branches to provide an absolute guarantee that, should the branch or the whole banking group be affected by a crisis, Community depositors will not be at risk.
5 If the Commission has the power to decide whether or not reciprocity is given by third countries to Community credit institutions, are the Member States going to accept peacefully the Commission's decisions?
6 Why are branches not covered by articles 8 and 9?

Article 10(1) states that a credit institution's own funds may not fall below the amount of initial capital. In order to reinforce the content of this principle, article 10(3) states that when a credit institution is taken by a person other than that who controlled the institution previously, the 'own funds' must attain the level of initial capital. The aim of this provision is to prevent promoters of a new bank preferring to take control of an existing bank without fulfilling the condition of initial capital requirement.

In article 10(4) there is an exemption to article 10(1): where there is a merger of two or more credit institutions, the 'own funds' of the institution resulting from the merger may not fall below the total 'own funds' of the merged institutions at the time of the merger. This is clearly a measure to facilitate the acquisition of a bank in crisis by healthy banks, and represents a kind of bounty favouring the healthy bank, since this provision does not require the fulfilment of the condition of initial capital.

Article 11 is a new provision. Although the First Banking Directive has a similar provision for bank managers (requiring them to be experienced and honourable), there is no mention of the shareholders which acquire (or have the intention of acquiring), directly or indirectly a qualifying holding in a credit institution. This article reinforces the feature of 'prudential supervision' in the Directive. The aim is to prevent the most important shareholders negatively influencing the sound and prudent management of the credit institution.

The content of article 11(3) which requires any person who proposes to dispose of a qualifying holding first to inform the competent authorities, was criticized by the German delegation during the Council discussions.[40] The German government's position should result in a more liberal procedure through the limitation of the arbitrary power of national authorities. In the words of the text proposed:

> ... les Etats membres ne doivent pas prévoir un contrôle général préalable des personnes visées à l'article 11(1) dans le cas oú celles-ci ne peuvent pas selon la situation du droit existant ou les clauses contractuelles exercer une influence négative sur la gestion saine et prudente de l'établissement de crédit ....[41]

Article 12 is one of the main provisions of the Directive. It incorporates rules requiring banks to fulfil certain objective criteria if they wish to acquire or maintain participation in non-credit or non-financial institutions. With these criteria the Directive aims to achieve adequate supervision in the interest of financial stability for two main reasons: first, because participation in a subsidiary may affect the soundness of a credit institution, if the former runs into financial difficulties (contagion risk); and, second, since equity participation constitutes a long-term freezing of the assets of credit institutions.

The positions of the Commission, the Council and the European Parliament varied in respect of the percentages which they allowed to the 'qualified participation' of the credit institutions in non-financial undertakings. The European Parliament, bearing in mind the role played by the banking system in the industrial and financial sector, recommends an amount of 25 per cent (own funds) and 75 per cent (qualified participation). The Commission opted in the first proposal for 10 per cent and 50 per cent respectively, but, after the EP's recommendation, raised the limit to 15 per cent and 60 per cent. The Council accepted this position but introduced some exceptions (articles 12(3) and (8)) in order to respect the position of countries with a 'universal banking system' (Germany, Spain, Greece and Holland). On the other hand, some countries (Belgium, Italy and France) where there is a general ban on this participation, opposed the introduction of these exceptions.[42] Once more, we are facing a provision with a high political content that could create insoluble structural problems for the weakest countries in the Community.

Articles 13, 14 and 15 contain the means of prudential supervision of a credit institution authorized in the EEC.

Article 13(1) is very important. By giving the competence of prudential supervision to the authorities of the home Member State, the article modifies changes the First Banking Directive's provisions on this issue.[43]

Article 14 states some exceptions to the rule set by article 13(1). Owing to the inadequate harmonization of the provisions regarding liquidity and, more generally, the lack of monetary cooperation, article 14(2) introduces an important derogation to the principle of supervision by the host Member

State. The host country retains primary responsibility for the supervision of the liquidity of credit institutions and complete responsibility for the implementation of monetary policy. These provisions show that, before the Single Market can be attained, the following are necessary: a more substantial convergence of the Member States' monetary policy, a precise description of its contents; and the continuation of efforts to harmonize national legislations in key sectors, such as the rules for calculating and supervising the liquidity of credit institutions. The smooth functioning of the internal banking market will require close and regular cooperation between the competent authorities of the Member States.

In Article 14(3) the Directive provides for cooperation between the relevant authorities of both the host countries and the home country to avert market risks resulting from operations by established credit institutions on the 'security markets'. Article 14(3) has become imperative, particularly in the light of the crash of the international stock markets on 19 October 1987 which demonstrated the fragility of the security markets, as well as the lack, in many Member States, of adequate measures. However, article 14(3) fails to specify the nature of these 'necessary measures' and the procedures for, and the extent of, cooperation among the competent authorities, both in this and in other instances covered by the Directive.

Perhaps it would be too ambitious to require the Banking Advisory Committee, under the ultimate supervision of the Commission, to assume a further essential and active role as a coordinator among the relevant authorities of the Member States in respect of all cases of cooperation, although this is urgently necessary. In this way, it could develop into a 'Community Banking Authority', which would undoubtedly be a positive contribution to efforts to set up a European Central Bank.

Article 15 provides for the possibility for home authorities, after first informing the host authorities, to undertake on-the-spot verification in branches of their credit institutions which are established in other Member States. The right to make on-the-spot verifications is recognized by the EC Commission for the protection of competition law. In this sense, it is interesting to compare the content of article 15(1) of the Second Banking Directive and article 7(1) of the First Banking Directive with article 7(a) and (b) of the 'antidumping regulation',[44] which raises several questions. Can the authorities of the host Member State deny its permission for the investigation? How much time must pass between the information and the undertaking of the verification?[45] How are the verifications going to be undertaken? What legal remedies can the workers of the branch to be investigated use for the protection of their professional rights?[46]

Article 16 deals with the question of 'professional secrecy'. Historically, this question has been only 'superficially' regulated by Community legislation as, for example, in Directives 77/799 (EEC), 79/1070 (EEC), 76/308 (EEC) and 79/107 (EEC) (harmonization of tax and VAT), and the First Banking Directive.[47] However, the Second Banking Directive significantly reinforces the existing Community provisions. The new obligations envisaged extend to:

- Article 16(1): Persons who now or in the past were employed by the competent authorities;
- Article 16(2): The exchange of information between the competent authorities of the Member States regarding matters of prudential supervision; and
- Article 16(3): The exchange of information provided in the context of a cooperation agreement between the competent authorities of a Member State and an authority of a third country.

Article 16(1) fills the gap in the definition of 'professional secrecy' and its consequences:

> … that no confidential information which they may receive in the course of their duties may be divulged to any person or authority what so ever, such that individual institutions cannot be identified, without prejudice to case covered by criminal law ….

This is an important innovation with respect to article 12 of Directive 77/780 EEC, and article 50 of Directive 85/611 EEC (UCITS) and is a direct consequence of the European Court's decision in case 110/84 '*Hillegom* v *Hillenius*',[48] which implicitly stated the necessity for such a definition.

Article 16(5) and 16(7) states two exemptions to the general rules of paragraphs 1 and 4. Article 16(5) uses the term 'authorities' which includes, according to Clarotti, '… dans les pays où ils existent comme par example la Grande Bretagne des organismes professionnels d'autocontrôle. …' Article 16(7) uses the expression '… authorize the disclosure of certain information to other departments …' which is translated by Clarotti as '… cette faculté s'étendre aux communications aux commissions parlementaires d'enquête. …'[49]

However, the 'professional secrecy' regulated by article 16 ignores the most important aspect: the relations between the bank and the customers. Whilst these relations are not regulated by the Community breaches of the principle of equal competition could appear within the EC as a function of the different regulations on 'professional secrecy' by Member States.

Article 18(1) constitutes the most important instrument towards achieving the principle of 'mutual recognition' of banking activities. This is complemented by the content of article 18(2) in which the subsidiaries of credit institutions are allowed to provide the activities listed in the Annex of the Directive throughout the territory of the Community if they fulfil several conditions provided for in paragraph 2. The reason for article 18(2) lies in the fact that, in some Member States, credit institutions are not allowed to carry out some of the activities listed in the Directive's Annex (as, for example, leasing, factoring, mortgage credit, safekeeping and administration of securities); only subsidiaries are allowed to do that. But subsidiaries are regulated by Directive 83/350, so they are not considered 'credit institutions' in the sense of Directive 77/780; therefore the activities which they carry out would not benefit from 'mutual recognition'.

Article 18 could cause some future, difficult legal and socioeconomic problems.[50] Socioeconomic problems could arise as a consequence of the different capabilities of national financial markets to absorb the new financial products recognized in the list. Although there is no doubt that the need for an efficient and dynamic banking system is greater in the underdeveloped countries and regions of the Community, the banking institutions of such countries and regions will not necessarily fall victim to a 'creaming off' process to the advantage of the large transnational banks.

Article 19 contains the forms of exerting the right of establishment. It is interesting to note the content of paragraph 4. The first part reads:

> ... before the branch of a credit institution begins its activities, the competent authorities of the host Member State, shall, within two months of receiving the information mentioned in paragraph 3, prepare for the supervision of the credit institution ....

The 'supervision' is understood to apply to the fields in which the host Member State conserves both principal and residual competence: the second part of paragraph 4 reads: '... and if necessary indicate the conditions under which, in the interest of the general good, those activities must be carried on in the host Member State'. The Directive gives no common definition of the meaning of 'general good'. Rosello tries to justify the absence of a 'list' to delimit the concept in the Directive, and gives some ideas of what we must understand by it:

> ... (a) the concept could be assimilated to the concept of mandatory rules in Private International Law. (b) It is necessary to make a restrictive interpretation of the concept, ignoring any form of administrative law or 'ius cogens' in it. (c) The delimitation of the concept is up to the European Court of Justice. Such a delimitation could be similar to that of the concept of 'general interest' enounced by the Court in case 205/84 (insurance), *Commission* v *Germany*: ...[51]

In any case, article 19 clearly states that, the host Member State cannot refuse the establishment in its territory of a branch of a credit institution duly agreed in its home member State.

Article 20 establishes a very simple procedure for the provision of services by a credit institution of one Member State within the territory of another Member State: the notification to the competent authorities of the home Member State of the activities on the list in the Annex which it intends to carry out. This article raises several questions. Why is the procedure much simpler than it is for the establishment of a branch? Would it not be better to give the home Member State the possibility of refusing the authorization for the same reasons as in article 19? Must we understand that the home Member State implicitly approves the provision of services in another Member State with the only condition of the notification by the credit institution? If this is what the article means, limits to the provision of services could only arise from the application by Member States of the 'safeguard clauses', provided for by Directive 88/361 EEC of June 1988 for the implementation of article 61(2) and 67 of the EEC Treaty (52).

Article 21 is another example of a political compromise between Member States made in order to respect the principle that the host Member State should take note of any irregular situation on the part of a credit institution and the home Member State should take the appropriate measures to ensure that the institution concerned corrects the irregularity.

Article 21(1) refers to credit institutions having branches within the territories of Member States, so there is no mention of the provision of services as such. This could mean that when a credit institution exercises the free provision of services (cross-border activities), there is no obligation to report on its activities to the competent authorities of the Member State where those activities are provided. This would also affect the content of article 21(2).

In paragraphs 4 and 8 host Member States are authorized to take appropriate measures when a credit institution persists in violating the legal rules referred to in paragraph 2. But these paragraphs are technically incomplete: there is no reference to the content and procedure of the measures that host Member States could take. Consequently, the content of these two paragraphs could provoke breaches to the 'principle of legal security' for the activities of credit institutions.

In paragraph 5 the concept of 'general good' is employed; the comments cited above also apply here.

Finally I should like to mention the content of paragraph 11 where credit institutions are allowed to advertise their services through all available means of communication in the host Member State. Surely this statement on the Directive is rather 'superfluous' when this fact has already been duly recognized by the Treaties and the jurisprudence of the European Court?[53]

Title V of the Directive must be read taking into account the content of article 8c (EEC Treaty) and the 'accession acts' of Greece, Portugal and Spain. These provisions state several stages before the achievement of freedom of establishment on 1 January 1993.

Article 22 gives 'executory powers' to the Commission in order to make technical adaptations to the content of the Directive. Executory powers have been recognized by the SEC to the Commission and has been delimited by the Council in its Decision 87/373 of 13 July 1987.[54] This decision stated that the Commission, on exercising its executory powers, has to act through three types of committee, one of which is the committee cited in paragraph 2 of article 22. This paragraph states that '... the Commission shall be assisted by a committee composed of representatives of the Member States ...'. As there is no specification of who can be appointed for this committee, Member States could appoint existing members of the Banking Advisory Committee – a situation which could render the existence of one of the Committees rather meaningless.

In article 22(1) subparagraphs 4, 5 and 6, the Commission is given executory powers which were the competence of the Council under the 'own funds' Directive of 19 April 1989.

Article 23 preserves the rights acquired by credit institutions providing services before the entry into force of the Directive, and also for branches which have commenced their activities in accordance with the provisions in force in their host Member States. It is worth noting that there is no reference to branches of credit institutions established outside the Community. It might therefore be suggested that a paragraph should be included in this article (as the Council did in its common position of the Directive in Solvency ratio)[55] in order to regulate the situation of those branches. With such a solution the Council would take another step on the way towards a 'common banking policy', by giving a communitarian regulation to a field which is still under the competence of the different Member States.

Article 24 constitutes an 'unusual' form of fixing the date for the bringing into force by Member States of the provisions of the Directive. Article 24(1) reads:

> ... to comply with the Directive by the later of the two dates laid down for the adoption of measures to comply with Directives 89/299 EEC and 89/647 EEC, and at the latest by 1th January 1993 ....

The only justification for the employment of such a '*formule de renvoi*' is that the implementation of these two Directives constitutes a fundamental 'first step' for bringing into force the provisions of the Second Banking Directive.

Supplementary Directives to the Second Banking Directive

Two further measures of vital importance for the achievement of essential aspects of the Second Banking Directive should be mentioned. They concern the definition of 'own funds' and the solvency margin of credit institutions.

The First Banking Directive expressly left the definition of own funds[56] (all those items which together constitute the capital of the bank) to the Member States' legislation, although the concept has been described as a 'cornerstone of banking supervision'[57] and the use of such a concept is practically essential for measuring and comparing capital adequacy.

Directive 89/299 EEC of 17 April 1989[58] now sets out common standards for the definition of own funds, which Member States are obliged to use in all their legislation implementing Community measures on the prudential supervision of credit institutions. The Directive distinguishes between original and additional own funds and limits the proportion which the latter may represent in the total.[59] It provides a maximum of items which can comprise own funds, along with a list of all those items which must be deducted from them. Member States may, however, allow the deduction of the other items. The net result is a Community minimum standard for the calculation of a bank's capital. The Directive also notes that '... the Member States ... shall be obliged to consider increased convergence with a view to a common definition of own funds' within five years of its implementation.[60]

Directive 89/647 EEC of 18 December 1989[61] sets out to provide a Community measure of the capital adequacy of credit institutions, to replace existing national regulations in this regard and to introduce a greater degree of comparability of supervisory standards. It should also strengthen the average solvency of Community banks, by better protecting depositors and investors from unforeseen difficulties.

Although the utility of ratios between assets and liabilities as an aid to monitoring solvency and liquidity of credit institutions was recognized in the First Directive,[62] the Commission's 1985 White Paper on completing the internal market does not mention a directive on solvency ratios. It may be assumed that the timing of this Directive owes something to the Proposals for the international convergence of capital measurement and capital standards put forward in December 1987 by the Basle Committee of banking supervisors of the Group of Ten, which includes seven Community

Member States.[63] The Directive will apply to all credit institutions which fall within the First Directive's definition. The solvency ratio itself – a mathematical concept – is defined as a credit institution's 'own funds [expressed] ... as a proportion of total risk-adjusted assets and off balance-sheet items'. From 1 January 1993, credit institutions will be obliged to maintain a solvency ratio to be calculated at least twice a year, at a minimum of 8 per cent, and to act as quickly as possible to restore the ratio to 8 per cent should it fall below this figure.

A large proportion of the text is devoted to classifying asset items according to their degree of risk expressed as a percentage, although Member States are permitted to prescribe higher weighting for them. Off-balance-sheet items are classified according to the Directive's three annexes. The total of the values of the assets and off-balance-sheet items thus adjusted for risk constitutes the denominator of the solvency ratio which must be maintained. Recent developments in the theory of finance suggest that balance-sheet controls are likely to impose small costs on society.[64]

Two administrative issues may, however, arise. First, because some banks may not be able to afford a high premium system, the risk-classification scheme should be as objective as possible. The system will only remain viable so long as there are no systematic errors in the setting of premiums.[65] Second, there is the question of whether the premium rates levied on individual banks should be publicly disclosed. This will obviously be opposed by high-risk banks, and by banks that may be threatened with a high-risk classification.

Finally, it should be noted that a 100 per cent insurance scheme solution – as a broader insurance coverage – would further reduce the likelihood of bank runs: in particular the possibility of a run by large depositors would be eliminated.

Notes

1 COM (87) 715 final, 16/2/1988.
2 See *Europe*, 14 January 1988, p. 5. See also P. Clarotti, 'Progress and Future Development of Establishment and Services in the EC relation to banking' JCMS, **XXII** (3), March 1984, pp. 225–6.
3 Case 120/78, 20/2/1979.
4 COM (87) 715, final page 4.
5 EC Commission, 'Research on the cost of non Europe' Financial Services, **9**, Luxembourg, 1988, p. 27.
6 See PE Text, 3/89.
7 See OJ, no. C 318/42 (12/2/88).
8 See *Europe* (4699) 14 January 1988, p. 7.

9 See chapter related to the European financial environment and its influence on the EC banking harmonization process.
10 Directive of 15/12/89; OJ, no. L 386/1 (30/12/89).
11 Council document 7835/89, published as EP DOL C3–16/89.
12 The Commission has adopted a similar approach in its proposal for a directive, submitted in January 1985, mortgage credit (OJ 1985 C 42/4).
13 See P. Clarotti, 'Un pas décisif vers le marché commun des banques', *Revue du Marché Commun* (330), September–October, 1989, p. 454. Also G. Zavvos, 'Towards a European Banking Act', *Common Market Law Review*, **25** (263), 1988, p. 271 and 'Interview with Mr J.L. Rosello (main administrator in GD 15 of the Commission CEE), 11 March 1990.
14 See p. 5 of 'restricted document', no. 7239/89 EF 54 (13/6/1989) Council of the EEC.
15 See Debauve: case 52/79 (1980); ECR 833.
16 OJ, no. L 266 (9/10/80).
17 Page 7 of 'restricted document' cited note 14 supra.
18 Page 9 of 'restricted document' no. SN/2331/89 (EF) (26/6/1989) Council of the EEC.
19 See 'Recent Innovations in International Banking', *Bank for International Settlements*, April 1986, pp. 240–1.
20 Page 10 of 'restricted document', no. 7239/89, cited note 14 supra.
21 COM (88), 718 final; OJ, no. C 43 (22/2/1989) presented to the Council by the Commission (3/1/1989).
22 See, White, 'Price Regulation and Quality Rivalry in a Profit-Maximizing Model: The case of Branch Banking', *Journal of Money, Credit and Banking*, February 1976, pp. 107–18. See also A.S. Carron: 'Reforming the Bank Regulatory Structure', Washington, 1984, p. 28.
23 Page 11 of 'restricted document' no. 7239/89, cited note 14 supra.
24 See P. Clarotti, 'Un pas décisif …' op. cit., p. 456.
25 Unger, Case 75/63; (19/3/1964). ECR, 1964; Levin, case 53/81; (23/2/1982). ECR, 1982.
26 Van Roosmalen, case 300/84 (23/10/1986); ECR, 1986 Dona, case 13/76 (14/7/1976); ECR 1976.
27 See page 14 of 'restricted document' no. 7239/89, cited note 14 supra.
28 Decisions: 27/6/1967, OJ 1967/163; 21/12/1973, OJ 1974/ L 191/18; 23/10/1975, OJ 1975 L 286/24; 11/12/1979, OJ 1980 L 39/73.
29 See H. Scott, 'In Quest of Reason: the Licensing Decisions of the Federal Banking Agencies', *University of Chicago Law Review*, **42** (235), 1975.
30 Rockoff, 'The Free Banking ERA: A Reexamination', *Journal of Money, Credit and Banking*, May 1974, pp. 141–68.
31 A. Posner 'The Social Costs of Monopoly and Regulation', *Political Economy*, **83** (4), August 1975, pp. 807–29.
32 S. Peltzman, 'Bank Entry Regulation: Its Impact and Purpose', *The National Banking Review*, December 1965, pp. 163–7.
33 N.A. Lash, *Banking Laws and Regulations: an Economic Perspective*, Prentice-Hall, 1987, pp. 36–9.
34 See P. Clarotti, 'Un pas décisif …' op. cit., p. 457.
35 See 'restricted document' no. 7239/89, cited note 14 supra.
36 COM (87) 75 final pp. 7–8.
37 See *European Community News*, 20 October, 1988, p. 4.

38 PQ no. 134/9 answered by Sir Leon Brittan, in OJ, EC, C, no. 233 of 17 September 1990, p. 16.
39 See H.S. Scott: 'La notion de réciprocité dans la proposition de deuxième directive de coordination bancaire', *Revue du Marché Commun* (323), January 1989, p. 47.
40 See p. 25 of 'restricted document', no. 7239/89, cited note 14 supra.
41 Ibid.
42 Ibid.
43 Giving Member States the faculty to establish an 'authorization procedure' for the branches of credit institutions whose head offices were in other EC countries.
44 Council Regulation no. 2423/88; (11/7/1988) OJ, no. L 209/1.
45 See, in this sense, I. Van Bael and J.F. Bellis (1989) *Competition Law of the EEC* (2nd edn), Oxford: CCH Editions Ltd (Paragraph 1003: Discovery, on the spot investigation, pp. 289–94).
46 It is worth noting the position *against* the content of article 15/11 by the Luxembourg delegation within the Council. See page 29 of 'restricted document' 7239/89, cited note 14 supra.
47 Article 12 of Directive 77/780.
48 Case 110/84, 11/12/1985 Recueil 1985, pp. 3947–66.
49 See P. Clarotti, 'La deuxième directive de coordination en matière de'ètablissements de crédit'; p. 461.
50 Ibid., p. 462.
51 *Recueil de la Jurisprudence de la Cour 1986*, p. 3755.
52 OJ, no. L 178 (8/7/1988) p. 5.
53 See also recent UCITS Directive, where marketing rules are stated as competence of the Member States.
54 Decision 87/373, EEC; OJ no. L 197 (18/7/1987).
55 Common position on 24/7/1989; EP Doc C3–17/89.
56 It has been suggested that this expression is a mistranslation of the French term *Fond propres*, and that 'banking capital' is to be preferred in English.
57 Explanatory statement to the Commission's proposal: COM (86) 169, final 2; p. 1.
58 OJ 1989 L 124/16.
59 Article 6 of Directive 89/299 EEC.
60 Article 2 (2) of Directive 89/299 EEC.
61 OJ, no. L 386/14 (30/12/89).
62 Article 6 of Directive 77/780 EEC.
63 It should be remembered that the Basle recommendations only apply to banks of a certain stature, and, in any case, are not binding on the participant states.
64 In particular, in a world of perfect capital markets, without taxes and without bankruptcy costs, the allocation of resources will be independent of the balance sheets adopted by firms for mandated by regulation. See Modigliani and Miller, 'The Cost of Capital, Corporation Finance, and the Theory of Investment'; **48**, *American Economic Review* (3), June 1958, pp. 261–97. For a similar view, see Mayer, 'Should Large Banks be Allowed to Fail?', *Journal of Financial* and *Quantitative Analysis*, November 1975; pp. 603–10.
65 See Scott and Mayer, 'Risk and Regulation in Banking: Some Proposals for Federal Insurance Reform', *Stanford Law Review*, **23**, May 1971, pp. 857–902.
66 See Barnett, Horvitz and Silverberg, 'Deposit Insurance: the Present System and Some Alternatives' *Banking Law Journal*, **94**, April 1977; pp. 304–32.

2 Conclusions

Several remarks can be made following critical approach to the harmonization process of banking activities in Europe.

Harmonization

The 'harmonization process' has enabled the Community to remove some of the long-outstanding backlog measures, rather than proceed to adopt those which are required by present conditions or will be required in the near future. Not only can it be maintained that in the area of financial services, which, it is recalled, represented some 7 per cent of the Community's GDP,[1] the Community has achieved too little, it may also be the case that this little is, in many cases, rather late. The change in the nature of banks' activities, for example, is a constant theme in the discussion of financial services.[2] The importance of a bank's credit risk, on which the traditional approach to prudential supervision was based, has diminished compared with exchange rate risks, interest rates risks and securities market risks. Yet there is no sign of a Community measure to deal with this modification in the financial ground rules.

Mutual Recognition

Concern has also been expressed that, although it has proved a useful lubricant for the legislative process, the technique of mutual recognition – a 'second best' compared to coordination of national provisions – gives rise to the danger that the interest of consumer–investor protection 'may be subordinated to the policy of speedy completion of the internal market' and encourage the Member States to accept the lowest common denominator in fixing the Community standard.[3] The approach based on the principle of equivalence, as proposed in the Commission's White Paper on *Completing the Internal Market of 1985* also raises concern. Both freedom of services and consumer protection at a high level would be served by imposing the standards of the country of origin in all countries where the services are marketed. All services would thereby be able to circulate freely within the internal market and be supervised by the authorities of the country of origin under certain standard conditions applicable, but not necessarily harmonized, Community-wide.

Prudential controls established on banking institutions in every Member State, and supervised by the home country authorities, will not be adequate to protect efficiently the consumer funds deposited in a credit institution against fraud and bankruptcy. Positive integration is required to provide for such assistance as a Community-wide obligatory guarantee-fund system,[4] or obligatory deposit insurance schemes and suchlike.[5] As Revel stated,[6] an approach to prudential regulations which relys on balance-sheet ratios – particularly if they are uniform across whole groups of institutions of different sizes and specialization – is a dead end. In a fast-changing financial system the essential feature of an effective system of prudential regulation is a concentration on the risk exposure of individual institutions, which cannot be achieved by detailed regulation. It demands a high degree of competence among the supervisors, whose attention should be concentrated on the doubtful cases.

Cross-border Transactions

Cross-border transactions put the individual consumer in a more vulnerable position towards its partner in terms of access to information and dispute settlement procedures. Private international law rules, when applicable, give consumers a far from adequate solution to the settlement of disputes arising in the context of cross-border transactions. The latter concern, for example: the conclusion of the contract (availability and presentation of the terms and conditions governing the transaction, marketing practises); change of contract terms; allocation of risks and liability rules in cases of system failure and payment to an unauthorized third party; documentary evidence and the assigning of the burden of proof; revocability of orders of payment; and error and dispute settlements procedures.

Banking services are subject to the Convention of Jurisdiction of 1968,[7] and the Convention on Contractual Obligations of 1980,[8] but exemptions are made possible which could allow the consumer not to be granted the most favourable provisions of the laws which would be declared applicable to his transaction.

Data Protection

New technological developments in financial services in the EC countries are taking place in a legal vacuum. Citizens have already voiced their concern on the use of computer systems and the invasion of personal privacy, by holding information on private individuals without their knowledge or consent, by disseminating this information to other institutions or persons, or by using computer systems to monitor individual behaviour. Electronic Fund Transfers Personal Offering Services (EFTPOS) offers specific and additional risks in terms of protecting the privacy of individuals using the system: data make it possible to trace the consumer in all his travels and places where purchases are made and to draw a clear profile of his consumption habits. Reference should be made to the provisions of the 1981 Council of Europe Convention for the Protection of Individuals with Regard to Automatic Processing of Personal Data.[9]

Removal of Financial Trading Barriers

The effect on the market of the international liberation of financial services is far from clear. While removal of barriers to international trade in financial services and to the international capital movement should lead to more competition, the related restructuring of the financial services industry may lead to higher concentration and anti-competitive arrangements. Competition at the international level will indeed require the constitution of 'financial conglomerates' through takeovers, mergers and agreements to use or exchange common network services. Forms of cooperation may include detailed agreements on technical standards, security measures, operating procedures, tarification rules and so on. They will also imply restrictive agreements between the financial institutions and retailers accepting the common payment system. Such a restriction of competition, while inevitable, should be contained within reasonable limits and should not lead to market structures and practices which would be directly detrimental to the consumer – namely, by imposing excessive prices and other unfair conditions, or by restricting the choice of payment methods available.

Another anti-competitive effect would result from attempts made, at EC level, to achieve a common market for financial services and simultaneously to create barriers against the rest of the world. The recent 'European Agreement for Bank Cards Usage' which has been drafted by the European Council for Payment Systems and notified to the Commission for a possible exemption from the application of the Treaty rules on competition is a good illustration of such protectionist behaviour, since it excludes from participation non-European banks and financial institutions.

Social Effects

Social policy is also omitted from the financial services harmonization process. Employee participation and company structure are questions of no easy solution which affect credit institutions. Some reflections from Pipkorn could be of interest here:

> '... a much broader attempt to realize the goal of an increasing participation of the employees in the life of their undertaking, laid down in the Community's social action programme of 1974, has been made with the Commission's proposal for a directive on procedures for informing and consulting employees of undertakings with complex structures in particular transnational undertakings'.[10]

The Commission has justified the need for a directive on this subject on the grounds that the decision-making process of large enterprises has become so complex that the existing procedures for informing and consulting employees no longer correspond to the level where decisions with serious repercussions for employees are taken. Such procedures are generally confined to the affairs of the local business entity and do not reach the level of the real decision-making centre in cases where this entity is legally an autonomous company, but economically a part of a group of companies under uniform management. For example, if the dominant undertaking of such a group is located in Germany, it would be informed on the decisions taken at group level in accordance with existing German legislation on group works councils, but the workers in the subsidiaries in Belgium or France need not be informed and consulted under this law, which has its territorial scope limited to Germany. The unequal treatment of employees affected by the decisions of one, single undertaking, stemming from this territorial limitation of existing information and consultation procedures, impedes the realization of the social goals set forth in article 117 and is inconsistent with the creation of conditions in the EC similar to those of a domestic market, as aimed at by the whole EC Treaty and specifically by articles 2, 7, 48 and 52 (11):

> ... The directives and draft directives dealt with so far aim at protecting the interests of the employees through procedures ensuring that they are properly informed prior to decisions affecting them and granting procedural arrangements for a dialogue between the decision-maker which determines de facto the employment conditions and the employees' representatives with respect to

'monitoring' the social consequences of such decision' .... The most controversial issue is the participation of employees in the election of the members of the governing bodies of companies ....[12]

Fiscal Issues

Fiscal issues are also at stake. As regards corporate taxation, a uniform taxation system should be necessary in order to avoid the problems of finding an uncontrolled market price for transfers between affiliated companies.[13] The above fiscal achievement will avoid situations such as that created by the *Daily Mail*[14] as regards capital gains taxation in the UK; neither the European Court nor the General Advocate could justify the transfer of the residence for tax reasons,[15] stressing the opinion maintained in several previous cases. This solution, though legally admissible, does not cope with the factual problem, inherent to every business profit-making mentality, that money looks for niches where it can maximize its value. Thus, credit institutions will develop strategies in order to place their financial products in countries where fiscal issues can easily be overcome.

As regards financial conglomerates, another issue to face is the criteria for defining business income. Quite aside from the question of tax rates, the criteria that regulate the classification of taxable income, the exceptions to the accrual principle, payment advances or deferrals, tax suspensions or payment instalments, cost allocation criteria and so on may have a weight significant effect on the overall structure of the tax levied.

Political Influence

The majority of Council's members were representatives of the Christian Democratic or Liberal parties,[16] and it is worth noting that the credit institutions may have close relations with these politicians. As we shall see in the following chapters, most of the latter are involved in activities closely linked to banking. The study of the strategies for the achievement of their objectives will also be analysed in subsequent chapters. The legal outcome of this situation has been a not very convincing set of rules included in the Commission's *White Paper for the Achievement of the Internal Market*.

If the Second Banking Directive is to be the 'cornerstone' for the creation of a single market for banking activities in Europe, it seems that many gaps have to be filled in order to avoid the house collapsing.

Notes

1 Fitchew, 'Vers un marché unique des services financiers', CDE symposium, Brussels, 27–28 April 1989, p. 1.
2 Delmas-Marzalet and Jozzo, *Proceedings of the 1986 symposium on 'Europe and the Future of Financial Services'*, pp. 3 and 133, respectively.
3 Remarks of Professor Gower to the Commission's 1988 Conference on Financial Conglomerates, pp. 5–12.
4 Such a system is proposed by the Commission in its draft directive of 21 March 1988 concerning 'package holiday tours', COM (88) 41 final (OJ, of 12/4/1988).
5 Such schemes have been introduced, but as an invitation only, in the text of the Commission Recommendation of 22 December 1986 concerning 'credit institutions' (OJ, no. L 33/1987).
6 See, J. Revell, 'Solvency and Regulation of Banks', *Bangor Occasional Paper in Economics* (5), University of Wales Press, 1975.
7 Convention of 27 September 1968 on Jurisdiction and the Enforcement of Judgements in Civil and Commercial Matters, OJ, no. C 97/1983.
8 Convention of 19 June 1980 on the Law application to Contractual Obligations, OJ, no. L 266/1980. This Convention has not yet been implemented in Belgium the Netherlands, Portugal and Italy.
9 OJ, no. C 297/1980, p. 3 published with an explanatory memorandum in EC Bulletin 3/1980 supplement.
10 J. Pipkorn, 'Employee Participation in the European Community: Progress and Pitfalls' in B. Wilpert and A. Sorge (eds), 1989.
11 Ibid., pp. 60–1.
12 Ibid., p. 68.
13 See T. Nielsen, 'The Arms's Length Test: a Rule of Law or an Excuse for Arbitrary Taxation?', *Interfax*, **296**, 1979. See also M. Burge, 'The 1975 U.K. Treaty as a Concrete Example of How Some Problems can be Handled' in *NYU International Institute on Tax and Business Planning 1977*, Tax Treaties and Competent Authority, New York, 1978.
14 *Daily Mail*, Case 81/87, 27 September 1988.
15 See cases: 27/01/83, Commission V. France, ECR 1986, 273; 115/78; Knoors ECR 1979, 399 and 33/74, Van Bisbergen, ECR, 1974, 1299.
16 The political composition of the Council on 15 December 1989 (date of the approval of the Second Banking Directive) was: Denmark, Germany, Portugal and the United Kingdom (right-wing governments), Belgium, Greece, Ireland, Italy, Luxembourg and the Netherlands (coalition governments composed of Socialist, Liberals, Christian Democrats, etc); Spain and France (Socialist).

PART II

THE WAY BANKS EXERCISE INFLUENCE WITHIN THE EC DECISION-MAKING PROCESS

3 A Short Review

> ... car, et nous insisterons tout particulièrement sur ce point, l'Europe que nous fabriquent les disciples de MM. Schumann et Monnet est, d'abord, celle des financiers et des hommes d'affaires.[1]

The above statement constitutes an introductory reflection to the study of the historical evolution of the influence of banks in the legal system of the Community. The EEC Treaty was born within a context of 'Pax Bancaria' (from the early 1930s to 1973), in which the main features were the high profitability of banking activities, light control on the part of the supervisory authorities, financial crisis without international consequences and so on. Scholars therefore seemed to reach a consensus in giving credit institutions the key with which to open the door of the integration process. Coston describes the 16-year period between the enactment of the EEC Treaty and the 1973 Directive as a period of time in which no other new measures were taken due to the needs of the credit institutions' internal politics.[2] It was only after the consolidation of the first stage (related to the basic conditions for the creation of the Common Market), that new objectives – both socioeconomic and financial – became an issue.[3] Lefour and Lagumina share the same view as regards the importance of market strategies based on 'concentration'.[4] Thus, it has been argued, the 1973 Directive was the consequence of several factors not necessarily linked to political or social aims: '... la *concurrence* des banques américaines et, *les besoins de financement* des sociétés multinationales ...'.[5]

The consequences of this pressure were reflected in both the quality and the quantity of the harmonization measures enacted by the Community. First, the only measure enacted by the Council, the 1973 Directive, clearly served the financial strategies adopted by the credit institutions. In fact, the principal objective of this Directive was the recognition of national treatment, which facilitated the above process of 'concentration' between the largest banks in the Community. Second, the 1971 and 1972 drafts of a European Banking Law[6] did not reach their final stage. Despite their highly technical content, and due to the wide range of objectives which they intended to regulate, the Banking Federation of the Community, (and the national banking organizations), pressed, together with the majority of the governments of the Member States, against the enactment of the projects.

The 1977 Directive, was merely a 'framework directive',[7] in which control was preferred to freedom. Thus the Directive summarized and unified measures in order to guarantee the financial soundness of the credit institutions after the 1973–75 economic crisis.[8] It is now generally agreed that the credit expansion of the early 1970s stimulated imprudent lending by banks, which in turn contributed to both the financial crisis of 1974 and the 1975–76 Great Inflation.[9] The 1977 Directive was thus the solution to problems which, although economic in origin, were also failures of supervision and regulation. The 83/350 and 86/635 EEC Directives,[10] were merely corollaries to this aim.

Roth notes the influence of credit institutions' strategies on the evolution of the harmonization process and states that business circles concerned with the provision of interstate services (that is, banking, insurance and the professions), have shown only a relatively limited interest in an expansion of the domestic markets to form a unified internal market.

> ... and that where such an interest in expansion exists, it is considered more advantageous to take the course of establishing branches and/or acquiring subsidiaries in the markets of the Member states concerned ....[11]

It can be assumed that not only complexity of the subject but also this lack of interest on the part of credit institutions is one reason why it has not been possible to reach more satisfactory results to date.

This view is shared by Roth when he states that, to date, the thrust of efforts to achieve coordination has been directed not so much at creating conditions for the exercise of an activity as at the development of mechanisms for cross-frontier administrative cooperation, with a strong shift towards the principle of home country control, accompanied by the mandatory recognition of certificates issued by the competent anthorities in the country of origin.[12]

Against this historical framework of the relations between the banks and the EC financial integration process, the question remains as to how banks influence this process, principally as regards measures related to the completion of the internal market.

Notes

1 *Revue d'Economie Politique*, special issue, January–February 1958, dedicated to the Common Market, presented by M. Jacques and edited by R. Courtin, P. Ori, F. Perroux *et al.*

2 H. Coston, *L'Europe des Banquiers*, Paris, 1965, pp. 24–5.
3 Ibid., pp. 25–6.
4 A. Lefour and A. La Gumina, 'Banques Europeennes: l'heure des rapprochements', *Entreprise*, **819**, 22 May 1971.
5 Ibid., p. 61.
6 FB CEE: *Cinquième Rapport (1971–72)*, Brussels, 1972, pp. 15–16; GC, CEE, *Rapport (1971–1972)*, Brussels, 1972, pp. 44–5.
7 See J.A. Usher, 'Financial Services in EEC Law', *ICLQ*, **37**, January 1988, pp. 148–9.
8 M. Porzio, 'Libera circolazione dei capitali e disciplina Communitaria delle banche', *Milano*, 1987, pp. 5 *et seq.*
9 See D. Laidler, 'U.K. Inflation and its Background: a Monetarist Perspective', in *Inflation in the U.K.*, Manchester: Manchester University Press, 1978, pp. 52–74.
10 OJ, 1983, L 193/18; OJ, 1986, L 372/1.
11 W.H. Roth, 'The European Economic Comunity's Law on Services: Harmonization, *Common Market Law Review*, **25** (35–94), 1988, p. 38.
12 Ibid., p. 48.

4 The Present Situation

I am now going to focus on the increasing activity of banks in order to adapt the measures envisaged for the completion of the internal market to their particular situation. In order to analyse more precisely the way through which pressure is brought, I have limited the research. First, only measures directly linked with the completion of the internal market are discussed. Second, only the Banking Federation of the European Communities at Community level is dealt with.

Aims of European Banks in Face of the Internal Market

The starting-point for the new banking legislation is the White Paper, which identifies six directives and two recommendations needed to complete the free movement of services in the banking sector. Since then, several more directives and recommendations have been added.

The Commission's approach towards achieving the liberalization of banking services is based upon three principles:

- introduction of a single licensing system for financial institutions permitting both the establishment of branches and the provision of services throughout the community;
- common rules on the supervision and regulation of financial institutions;
- the principle of home country control.[1]

These are the basis of the understanding between the Commission and the banks, which constitute the principal support of Commission's aims.

Nevertheless, the most important issue is to establish the exact degree of harmonization required by the rules of supervision and regulation of financial institutions. Here, everything depends on particular legislative traditions, but also on the material conditions of banks. The cleavage between those advocates of a low-key approach may be explained by a double axis. The first axis would oppose banks coming from a culture with a high degree of economic freedom (of which the UK is the clearest example) and banks coming from a mercantilist culture, characterized by a high degree of regulation and governmental intervention, (as in France). The second axis would oppose the most obsolete banks, which only survive by grace of national restrictions and which charge excessively high prices for their services. In general, we could allocate the British, Luxembourg and German banks to the first group and the Italian, French and, particularly, the Greek and Portuguese banks to the second one.

The 1992 Single market challenge will result in a drop in prices of at least 10 per cent (in some countries, such as Italy and Spain, of almost 50 per cent), and an increase in competence.[2] Obviously, these conditions will lead inevitably to a turmoil in the banking sector, which implies more bank failures and hostile takeover bids. As a consequence of these new circumstances, several governments, which are currently united in their desire for a more dynamic banking and financial services sector, now do not want the greater turmoil and risk which will accompany it and are pressing for increased regulation and protection against non-EC banks. In the near future, banks which feel unprepared for the new challenge, may demand more regulation, but, currently, they are still engaged with the Commission's plans. They are making demands to their own governments to prevent the excess of regulation and intervention which could place them in an adverse position vis-à-vis other European banks.

In the financial services sector, a great advance has already taken place – namely the decision to free capital movements, which will constitute the main foundation of the free movement of financial services. In addition, every Directive foreseen in the White Paper has been presented by the Commission to the Council.

Consequently, the work of banking lobbies concerning the Single Market is almost complete, and now only deals with questions of timing. The banks' interest in the single market is now focused on activities aimed at securing a good position before 1992,[3] and this affects mainly private activities and national reglamentation. Thus, the banking lobby's interests at EC level are being displaced to new areas such as consumer protection and payment systems.

The Second Banking Directive

There were many objections and difficulties of interpretation set down by banks. These principally concerned the definition of the term 'credit institution', the list of business which is integral to banking and shall be included within the scope of mutual recognition, third-country institutions and participation in non-banking sectors.

The Directive uses the definition of 'financial institution' set down by the First Directive (77/780/CEE). The banks demanded an extended definition, based on a functional criterion, arguing that the existing narrow definition provokes discrimination among banks and other institutions carrying our similar activities. According to the banks,[4] those demands were duly taken into account in the Commission's preliminary project, but reverted to the definition of the First Directive in the final version of the Commission's proposal.

Banks have also asked for an extended list of activities which are submitted to the principle of mutual recognition. They wanted services of investment banks, assurances brokerage, etc. to be included. This demand has not been taken up either by the Ecosoc, or by the Commission.

One of the main features of the debate was the problem of reciprocity concerning third countries' institutions. The banks asked for a clearer reciprocity clause, with the aim of obtaining the same conditions for community institutions in third countries by delaying the licence until the verification of reciprocal treatment in the home country of the third institution. This demand was taken up by the Ecosoc,[5] which articulated it by restricting the access of non-EC institutions to the single market of financial services. This coincidence of points of view was due to the fact that the conveyor of the banks' recommendations concerning the Second Directive was a certain M.J. Pardon, Director of the Belgian Banking Association and representative of the banks in the Ecosoc.[6]

Additionally, there was a great controversy concerning the proposal's intention to limit the banks' participation in the non-banking sector. The text's provisions would impose a limit on a bank's participation in a particular commercial or industrial undertaking to 10 per cent of their own funds. The reason behind this was that the banking authorities responsible for the supervision of the bank's activities would not be in a position to assess the risks of such ventures. However, the positions of banks varied according to their home countries. German banks are very heavily involved in such participations, while bank participation in non-banking sectors is prohibited in Italy and Belgium. Since it was impossible to find a compromise solution within the Federation, this allowed the national institutions to express openly their positions.

The Spanish banking association had the faculty to push towards a greater limit and has done it. The results of its pressure, added to that of other national associations, have been positive, resulting in the EP approval of an amendment increasing the limits laid down in the Directive to 20 per cent and 60 per cent respectively.

The approved Directive has finally established the limits on credit institutions' participation in non-credit and non-financial institutions at 15 per cent and 60 per cent (for an undertaking of, and for the total value of, non-banking participations) although member countries can choose whether or not to apply such limits to insurance companies.

Both the German and the Spanish banking associations applied strong pressure on the European Parliament. The case of the Spanish banking association highlights the importance pressurizing the EP in obtaining such an increase in limits. However, the German government also maintained a strong position in favour of such an increase until the approval of the Directive, even threatening to withhold approval of the Commission's proposal.

Banks' own funds must not fall below the initial capital required, although national authorities may allow a bank to restore its level of own funds after a certain delay. The condition which required all banks affected by the Commission's proposals to arrive at the level of initial capital of 5 million Ecus before 31 December 1996 has been substituted by a 'standstill' clause in the approved Directive.

The core of the Directive is contained in Title IV (articles 18–21) devoted to 'provisions relating to freedom of establishment and freedom to provide services'. Those articles establish the scope of mutual recognition, organize cooperation between the competent authorities of the Member States, and set up the procedure for the establishment and provision of services in the host country. Thus, the internal market (including 'home country control') principles are included in the said articles. Since no banking association has made any demands concerning these principles, articles 18 to 21 have passed unchanged through all of the decision-making procedures. This demonstrates the strong consensus between the Commission, the Member States and banks to implement the internal market for financial services – any outstanding differences are restricted to the definition of the proposed internal market's characteristics.

Bank Accounts

The Second Banking Directive claims to harmonize the form and contents of the annual accounts of banks and other financial institutions. By the time the White Paper was published, two of the Commission's proposals had already been presented. Directive (86/635/EEC) was adopted on 8 December 1986: agreement between banks and authorities, and on awareness of its necessity in order to complete the internal market allowed its adoption earlier than expected.

Bank Branch's Accounts

The White Paper anticipated a Directive concerning the accounts of banks' foreign branches. According to it, Member States are no longer able to oblige branches of banks whose headquarters are in another Community country to publish separate accounts. Branches will only have to supply the supervisory authorities with copies of the annual report and accounts drawn up by their head office, in accordance with the Directive on the Annual Accounts of Banks. Since this Directive fulfils an important and long-standing demand of European banks, its adoption has been welcomed by them.

This Directive was formally adopted by the Council on 13 February 1988, after the cooperation procedure. It does not differ substantially from the Commission's initial proposal of 1986, and reviewed in 1988.[7]

Mortgage Credits

The White Paper anticipated a Directive on the freedom of establishment and the freedom to supply services in the field of mortgage credit to be taken by 1988. The Commission's proposal was modified in May 1987 in order to take into account the amendments proposed by the EP.

The aim of the proposal is to abolish 'all institutional and technical provisions preventing or obstructing a credit institution from undertaking mortgage business throughout the Community'.[8] The Commission took the approach that an approximation of the existing regulation would be a cumbersome exercise and that it would serve no purpose. Because of this, it now proposes the solution of initial recognition, whereby each country must allow credit institutions from other Member States to apply their own domestic techniques in its market, even if such techniques do not comply with the rules of the host country.

The banks rejected this approach and demanded a harmonization concerning consumer protection measures, certain monetary measures and special banking system particularities. Their opposition was mainly directed against articles 4 and 5 – the key provisions of the Directive. However, this opposition has not been very successful since the amendments considered by the Commission have only a limited scope, and most of them are only improvements in presentation and in drafting.

More specifically, the Commission has kept the provision obliging Member States to authorize the credit institution which has suffered a distortion of competition due to the introduction (importation) of new financial techniques or equivalent measures. Banks argue that this provision in fact means a harmonization on the basis of less restrictive provisions, and that it is contrary to the Single European Act which requires a high level of protection for consumers. Perhaps national representatives in the Council will be more sensitive to these demands concerning consumer protection.[9]

The Reorganization and Winding-up of Credit Institutions

This Directive falls within the scope of the Council's work on the draft Convention on bankruptcy, winding-up, arrangements, compositions and similar proceedings. But the Commission had proposed that a Directive coordinating the role of bank supervisory authorities in these proceedings was necessary to apply it to the credit institutions. The Council working group responsible for finalizing the text of the Convention has recognized this was justified.[10]

The proposal was based on the principles of unity and universality. The principle of unity corresponds to the principle of home country supervision. The principle of universality is in line with that recognized by the Second Banking Directive, as regards the free provision of services contained in its annex.

In the amended proposal[11] the Commission has taken into account several demands of the EP concerning the strengthening of schemes to protect depositors. The proposal therefore now also includes a part of the Recommendation on the Establishment of a Guarantee System of Deposit within the Community, envisaged in the White Paper. This Recommendation was adopted by the Commission on 22 December 1986 (Recommendation of the Commission 87/63/EEC).

The proposal in now awaiting the Council's common position following the European Parliament's first reading.

The Harmonization of the Concept of Own Funds

In September 1986 the Commission presented the proposal of a Directive on the harmonization of the concept of own funds, originally envisaged as a recommendation in the White Paper. Although the Banking Advisory Committee, when consulted, suggested that a recommendation would be the appropriate instrument, the Commission decided that the definition of own funds is 'a cornerstone for much of the further work in the banking sector',[12] and consequently decided to propose a Directive.

The Commission revised this proposal in order to take into account the amendments proposed by the European Parliament, and the opinion of the Economic and Social Committee. The result was the amended proposal of 15 January 1988 (CM (88) 15 final).

After the lobbying carried out before the first proposal, the banks applied additional pressure in order to achieve a greater similarity with the orientation of the Bale Committee, but have not achieved important changes, in particular concerning the securities of indeterminate duration which banks wanted to be regarded as primary capital. After its second reading, the European Parliament rejected the 'common position' reached by the Council at the December Finance Council meeting, because of a problem of *comitologie*. Due to the fact that this common position was reached by unanimity, the Directive was unanimously approved by the Council on 17 April 1989 without any substantial change.

Solvency Ratios

The solvency ratios Directive, closely linked to the own funds Directive, has great significance in the light of the desire to permit credit institutions to provide services in Member States other than those in which they have their headquarters, under home country supervision. The Directive aims to strengthen average solvency standards among Community credit institutions in order to protect both depositors and the stability of the banking system.

The proposal of the Commission, presented in April 1988 (COM (88) 149 final), was lobbied by the banks. Their main objective, according to the Federation, was to prevent the national authorities being given the possibility of prescribing ratios above those fixed in the Directive. This possibility, which was envisaged in the Commission's first documents, effectively disappeared in the proposal. On the other hand, the banking lobby was unable to persuade the Community authorities to reduce the weighting of 50 per cent on the loans to individuals for the purchase of residential property, which, it argued, was excessive.

Banks which, according to national standards, maintain a high solvency ratio will not bear the drop of profitability that banks which have to increase their solvency ratio will have to afford. Third-country banks, mainly offshore, could benefit from lower solvency ratios, which would reduce their need for capital.

The solvency ratios Directive was approved on 18 December 1989 by the Council of Finance Ministers (Ecofin) after some '*comitologie*' disputes and some technical changes.

Control of Large exposures by Credit Institutions

This recommendation has merited little attention from banks and national authorities because of its non-obligatory character and because of the big margins left to the credit institutions and concerning large exposure. The recommendation of the Commission 87/62/CEE was adopted in December 1986.

Other Measures

Out of the directives and recommendations envisaged in the White Paper, there are many other measures which are objectives of banks' pressure. We can divide them into two groups: measures concerning non-banking sectors, but having significant implications for banks, and measures derived from the White Paper programme.

Among the different measures, the following are particularly important.

Legislative proposals for the final stage of the liberalization of capital movements These include: the proposal for a Directive for the full liberalization of capital movements; the proposal for the amendment of the 1972 Directive on the regulation of international capital flows; and the proposal for a regulation amending and combining the existing two Community instruments which are available to provide medium-term balance of payments assistance.[13] This programme means that one of the aims which inspired the creation of the BFEC has now been achieved. Because of this, the banks have strongly supported the Commission in this area.

Fiscality This is an area in which the Federation is making a big effort, including a detailed study about the incidence of VAT on financial activities. The Federation's is demanding the authorization to charge VAT on their financial products by an amendment of article 13 of the sixth VAT Directive, which allowed national legislation to decide over this faculty. The Commission has not considered this demand, but, on the contrary, has proposed the suppression of this right of national legislative option, in line with its programme to suppress fiscal barriers.

However the AEB (Asociación Española de Banca – Spanish Bankers Association) is strongly opposed to the demand of the Federation and several national associations (neither any Federation document, nor any people interviewed in the Federation mentioned this discrepancy).

Concerning the fiscality of capital the BFEC has been unable to arrive at a unanimous answer to the demand of a single position, in the light of the Commission's proposal ('Creation of a European financial area'; 4/11/1987, COM (87) 550 final). This demonstrates yet again the difficulties in obtaining a common decision in the BFEC, due to the fact that banks' positions rely on nationality, and everyone tries to maintain its existing national regulation.

The proposal concerning the definition of common technical features of the machines used to produce the new payment cards This proposal, envisaged in the White Paper in the chapter on new technologies and services, has been largely contested by banks on the grounds that an excess of regulation would hinder new advances in such a changing field. The Commission has been sensitive to these arguments and has consequently decided to transform the envisaged directive to a recommendation.[14]

The proposal for a directive on insider trading[15] This proposal, which has been recently adopted as Council Directive (89/592)[16] was supported by banks, but is also perceived as a possible constraint for operating in the financial market if it results in an excess of regulation.

The Commission Proposal of the Electronic Funds Transfer Directive One of the most important actions, in which we can appreciate the negative attitude of banks towards higher degrees of consumer rights protection, has been their opposition to the Commission Proposal of the Electronic Funds Transfer Directive.[17] Both the Commission and the BEUC (Bureau Européenne des Unions des Consommateurs) rejected the banks' argument that the proposal endangers future technological developments on the subject. The proposal is intended to remove responsibilities from the owner of an electronic payment card who uses it regularly and could be subject of illicit transactions, and will fix a unitary regulation on the subject. In fact, Denmark is the only Member State which has enacted a regulation protecting these consumer interests.

The interest of banks is considerably larger than that described here, and extends to other measures. However, their main effort is directed into the areas which we have dealt with.

The Objectives of Banks' Pressure

The main Community objective which European banks wish to influence in order to achieve their aims is the legislative process. This means pressurizing the four Community bodies involved in that process: The Council of Ministers which adopts the decisions; the Commission which has wide powers to submit proposals; and two consultative institutions, the European Parliament – a political body representing the citizens of Europe – and the Economic and Social Committee – a socioeconomic body representing social and economic interest groups within the Community.

The Council of Ministers

As mentioned before, the Council of Ministers is the most powerful single institution in the Community's structure, but it is, at the same time, the most difficult to permeate. Direct representations to the Council are not easy to arrange and may not be the most appropriate way of gaining the attention of Community Ministers and diplomats. A more indirect approach, by lobbying government departments in the national capitals may produce better results.

The Council of Ministers has the final word in most decisions. Its deliberations are extensive and crucial to most of the proposals that are placed before it. But all Council meetings are held in secret, the agendas are rarely made public in advance and access to the Council as a body is almost impossible for those who wish to press their claims and concerns. Few times does the BFEC ever get the chance to meet the Council of Ministers, even informally.

The objective that the Banking Federation of the European Community (BFEC) can hope to achieve at the Council of Ministers stage in the Community's decision-making process is to find out what is happening behind the Council's closed doors. The contacts that they have been able to build up over time in Brussels are with diplomats in the Permanent Representations – officials of the Commission that participate in the Council of Minister's discussions – and with journalists reporting Community business. Through them the BFEC obtains information about the negotiating stances adopted by each member, the main points of difficulty, and the possible compromises and trade-offs that are being floated. The BFEC must ensure also that their officials are on hand, in the corridors outside the meeting rooms, for any government official to consult if he so desires.

However, what the BFEC discovers about the secret discussions in the Council can prove to be vital leads to the nationally-based pressure groups which together comprise the BFEC's membership. The most effective lobbying almost invariably takes place in the national capitals, where national pressure groups have to lobby. These officials will themselves be happy to obtain the reactions of the main national parties to a particular Community proposal. The more technical the nature of the proposal, the more government officials are lobbied by the BFEC, once the Council of Ministers' negotiations begin.

Most of the work at the Council of Ministers stage is done in the working groups convened specifically to look at individual proposals within the Committee of Permanent Representatives (COREPER). Each Member State is entitled to send a delegation of between three and five people to each working group meeting. Such a delegation would typically comprise one person from the Ministry of External Affairs, and one person from each of the functional ministries or government agencies with an important interest in the subject matter. The External Affairs representative will commonly be drawn from the ranks of those it has posted in Brussels at its Permanent Representation. The working groups will begin a cycle of meetings, depending on the availability of rooms and interpreting facilities, on a monthly or bimonthly basis. Frequently, these experts find it difficult to resolve their conflicts and, when deadlock is reached, the matter will be referred to COREPER for a political solution thrashed out by the diplomats. If detailed technicalities have to be understood before a workable compromise can be put forward, then COREPER will pass the problem to an ad hoc committee of attachés from the Permanent Representations. A particular draft piece of legislation may pass backwards and forwards between COREPER, the working groups and the ad hoc committees several times before an outline agreement is reached. At this stage, the BFEC are very much on the outside of the decision-making process, and only those with very close relations with the officials involved can expect to have information about it.

When the working groups come up with a text which they can recommend to COREPER for approval, the job of the latter is to narrow the areas of disagreement down to the political level of government ministers. When the full Council of Ministers meets, Ministers will find many measures for decision on their agendas, and only matters starred 'B' will be discussed in detail at this level.

We will see later how banks do exert pressure in such an important Community institution. We will also consider my previous statement that there is little scope for direct lobbying because the Council meetings are still held in the manner of an international conference, with decisions being taken, in many areas, behind doors and out of the public view. However, the national interest groups have opportunities to exert influence via national ministers or other national representatives all through the Council's negotiation process.

The European Commission

As previously mentioned, there are considerable opportunities to lobby the Commission. Over the past 15 years, the Commission has sought the support of interest groups in order to strengthen its position within the Community. Also, the Commission and European pressure groups need, and use, one another as an information source. The BFEC, and frequently national pressure groups too, need to obtain information from the Commission about its policies and operations and about its future plans. Through access and the opening of bilateral relations, the BFEC hope to influence the attitude and behaviour of Commission officials whose work touches on their own field of concern. The Commission, for its part, needs information about the variety of positions and aspirations of the BFEC and national pressure groups, as well as factual information which may be slow in arriving from national government sources.

There are also wider reasons for the Commission's friendly stance towards pressure groups. The Commission wants to extend the Community's influence below the level of national governments, which are its principal interlocutors in the EC decision-making process. In addition, the Commission and pressure groups may, at times, find it is mutually beneficial to bypass the national government level on issues on which national governments are not prepared to give ground. In any case, the Commission will, as a matter of policy, always prefer to talk to the BFEC with an agreed viewpoint than have to discuss the same topics separately with national pressure groups.

These closed relations between the BEFC and the Commission are explained in that power of initiative already mentioned. The EEC Treaty in particular not only calls upon the Commission to flesh out specific common policies, but also to develop other policies which give effect to the principles laid down in the Treaty. So, in practice, the Commission's duties extend far beyond the role that is traditionally assigned to the civil service in each Member State: it has not only an administrative role but a political one as well.

However, policy initiation is not the only task the Commission has to undertake; it also has substantial powers in the field of the management and enforcement of existing policies – areas which can be of equal interest to the BFEC. The Commission can take independent action to enforce Community laws and obligations without needing the approval of the Council. And, in some areas, the Commission has been given delegated powers by the Council – for example, in the application of the competition policy.

The Commission makes particular use of so-called experts in many aspects of its work, and the BFEC may well be able to advise a Commission official in his search for outside expertise. This is an excellent way of contacting the Commission. However, the main problem for the BFEC is to know where to find the relevant officials. Incoherent and inconsistent policy stances can easily emerge from the Commission because directorates-general make policy decisions separately, rather than jointly. The interests of the Commission's directorates-general frequently overlap and responsibilities often do not fall clearly into the lap of just one directorate-general. Battles then won by the BFEC in one directorate-general can all too easily be blocked by another.

In the case of European banks' interests, they are mainly dealt within the following directorates-general: DG1 (external relations); DG2 (economic and financial affairs); DG3 (internal market and industrial affairs); DG4 (competition); DG11 (consumer protection); and DG15 (financial institutions and taxation). The European banks must maintain occasional contact with these six departments. Obviously, their main contacts at a technical level are with DG15. However, the banks' additional community interests must be reflected in contacts with DG1; when the dominant issue is freedom of establishment for banking institutions there must be contacts with DG4; and the increasingly important subject of the vigilance of the quality of banking services explains the contacts with DG11.

The European Parliament

In an initial and approximate approach to the question of the role of lobbies in the EP, two apparently contradictory ideas are frequently repeated: members of the EP are not a relevant target of pressure, and EP policy-making is strongly dependent on European and national lobbies. This feeling, especially perceivable among the Commission's officials, must be analysed

Concerning the first idea, there are two reasons which can explain the lobbies' lack of interest on the EP: its lack of power and, specifically, its inability to identify specific strategic political objectives commanding a consensus throughout the Parliament. However, its growing political influence and the importance the Parliament has in the Community budget are increasingly making it a focal point of the BFEC. After the direct elections and, moreover, after the procedure modifications introduced by the Single European Act, the BFEC is turning to the EP.

The BFEC is principally lobbying the EP because of its budgetary power and its ability to influence the Commission, especially when cooperation procedure is followed. Also important are the EP's ability to mobilize support and its ability to force the Commission to pay attention to a certain point. However, the EP is also interested in making contact with the BFEC. According to Kirchner[17] there are two reasons why the EP needs the BFEC's support:

a to obtain specialised information from the BFEC and to draw on the expertise of the BFEC; and
b to secure satisfactory consultation with the BFEC, specially on budgetary questions, in order to draw on the BFEC as a source of support or to win it as an ally vis-à-vis the Council.

Thus, it can be seen that the EP has a developing role as a target for the BFEC activities. This trend will continue if, as seems feasible, the EP continues to increase its powers.

In the field of community action with which my research deals, the importance attached by the BFEC to the EP should be considerable, because the cooperation procedure is followed in all measures envisaged in the White Paper, thanks to article 100A.

The second idea is that of the EP's dependency on interest groups in general and the BFEC in particular. There is a general trend to perceive all Western European parliaments as the main avenue of expression of interest groups. The decline of the national parliaments' role in modern policy-making is transforming them into fora of discussion, in which interest groups have to intervene.

However, in national parliaments the outcomes of policy decisions continue to be controlled by political parties, which have increased their strength, while in the European Parliament the weakness of political groups causes its political outcomes to be perceived as determined by the will and ability of strongest lobbies. The excessive dependency of the EP on the main interest groups is noted by many Commission bureaucrats. Recently, in a private conversation, a former member of the Commission expressed this idea, based, according to him, in the lack of sufficient information held by the members of the EP and their ability to collect it.[18]

This argument is rejected by Europarliamentarians. According to a Spanish parliamentarian, head of his political group in the EP, the European Parliament is the most powerful parliament as regards access to information, thanks to its ability to obtain it from the Commission and the Council and thanks to the high level of the parliamentarians' background.[19]

The methods used by the BFEC to penetrate the EP may be divided into two groups, according to Sidjanski[20]: the first is to penetrate inside the EP, helping certain representatives of the interest groups to be elected; the second consists in a group of actions, trying to influence EP outcomes.

The first way is very often used in the EP, specially within several political groups, such as a Gaullist one. The financial and banking sector is especially well represented, principally among British, Benelux and Italian parliamentarians. The actions developed by the BFEC are: studies or surveys; letters or direct contacts; and institutional declarations. A notable form of access is through the mass media, even though banks use this method only infrequently.

In this field of actions, banking lobbies encounter an additional obstacle, due to the poor image usually associated with the influence of big banks. Many parliamentarians carefully avoid displaying their relationships with the representatives of banks, for fear of being perceived as spokesmen for capitalists.

The pressure objectives of interest groups are individual EP parliamentarians, groups and committees. The work of the banking lobbies is based on selective relations, because they are only concerned with certain decisions within a limited field. These lobbies, as well as others of the same size, tend to have contacts mainly with certain political groups, EP committees or selected '*rapporteurs*'.

Banking interest groups mainly have contacts with individual members of the EP. The particular structure of the EP, in which there is no strict party discipline, renders the MEPs the most important pressure-group target. Obviously, the easiest contacts are with MEPs with a banking background who belong to the Liberal or the Democrat groups.

The banking lobbies are specially interested in the works of Economic and Monetary Affairs Committee, which intervenes in the debates on all the directives proposed in the White Paper, which are submitted to the cooperation procedure.

Direct contacts between banking lobbies and parliamentarians rely almost exclusively on the activities of national interest groups. The Banking Federation has, however, contacts with them as we will see.

The Economic and Social Committee

The main function fulfilled by the Ecosoc is not contained in the Treaties. It is to create relationships between the EC institutions and the economic groups of the member countries. The Ecosoc favours consensus among different economic interests and gives a more practical approach to the measures envisaged by the Commission. It also serves to help the BFEC to reformulate their demands from an European perspective. It could be said that the Ecosoc is the 'natural' way for the BFEC to express their demands and, because of this, they attach great importance to it.

The members of the Ecosoc are personally named and cannot receive any imperative mandate. However, because of the small importance accorded by the other institutions to the Ecosoc's opinions, many chiefs of credit institutions have been replaced by managers and high-level employees, which implies a loss of independence.[21]

Other Community Institutions

The European Court of Justice The legal work of the Court of Justice which interprets the law in full independence, often creating new laws or developing existing ones, is closely monitored by representatives of the

BFEC. There are no representations of European or national groups at the European Court of Justice, but several chairmen of the Ecosoc have visited the Court of Justice in Luxembourg.

Representatives of the BFEC deny any attempt to lobby judges of the European Court, whose independence is guaranteed in the Treaties. However, some kind of indirect pressure is applied, concerning certain causes, by means of the intervention which Commission and Member States can make in every case. The BFEC can lobby those Member States or the Commission in order to present before the Court the intervention they want.

The European Council The lobbying of this body shows how the major European interest groups make their presence felt whenever they have even a slight possibility of exerting influence at the European level. This influence is mainly exerted by the BFEC through the relatively regular meetings held by the President before the meeting of the European Council.

The European Investment Bank Since the EIB is an instrument of European structural policy and has a significant influence on the granting of funds, banks in particular may have certain interests in having contacts with it. However, these contacts are never made through the banking associations.

Notes

1 Commission of the ECs: 'Completing the internal market: an area without internal frontiers. The progress report required by article 8B of the Treaty' COM (88) 650, final, 17 November 1988.
2 Research on the 'Cost of Europe', Basic Findings: Vol. 9, 'The Cost of non-Europe' in *Financial Services*, Commission of the European Communities, March, 1988.
3 Ibid.
4 *Rapport annuel FBCE*, November 1986–December 1987.
5 Avis du Comité Economique et social sur la Proposition de deuxième directive.
6 See also *Briefing*, Brussels: Norton Rose, 1990.
7 Proposals COM (86) 396 final and COM (88) 118 final.
8 'Proposal for a council directive on the freedom of establishment and the free supply of services in the field mortgage credit', COM (84) 730 final, 24 January 1985.
9 Spanish banks accord great importance to these demands of the Federation since a swift opening of national mortgage credit market would imply the disappearance of Spanish banks from this market, due to their underdeveloped techniques. So they are pressing, alongside the Federation, to avoid the total rapid liberalization envisaged by the Commission.
10 Text adopted during the second reading on 5 August 1983 (Council document No. 8659/83 DSR 38).

11 COM (88) 4 final.
12 'Proposal for a council directive on the own funds of credit institutions', COM (86) 169/2 final, 15 September 1986, Explanatory memorandum, p. 3.
13 See Communication from the Commissions 'Creation of a European financial area', COM (87) 550 final, 4 November 1987.
14 Interview with a medium-top-level official of DG 15.
15 Amended proposal presented by the Commission: COM (87) 1165 final.
16 EURONOT-138, 7 September 1988.
17 E.J. Kirchner, 'The European Parliament and Interest Groups' in R. Hrbek *et alia* (eds), *The EP on the Eve of the Second Direct Election: Balance Sheet and Prospects*, Brugges: Tempelhof, 1984. Kirchner adds a fourth reason (learning from them) which looks obsolete, due to the new developments in the EP powers.
18 Interview with Mr Rosello, DG 15.
19 E. Punset, Spanish member of the Economic and Monetary affairs Committee of the European Parliament.
20 D. Sidjanski 'The European Parliament and Interest Groups', op. cit.
21 Interview with Mr Jean Pardon, member of the Ecosoc and *rápporteur* of the Ecosoc report on the Second Banking Directive.

PART III

THE EC BANKING HARMONIZATION PROCESS IN THE LIGHT OF THE GLOBALIZATION OF FINANCIAL MARKETS

5 Introduction

The third part of this book is divided into three chapters. Chapter 6 is devoted to both the study of the current international economic context and its interrelationships with the shaping of the regulatory framework as regards banking activities in Western countries. Chapter 7 is dedicated to the study of the credit institutions' strategies towards the achievement of a regulatory environment which could afford them the most suitable framework for developing their business projects. Finally, Chapter 8 takes a critical approach to the regulation of financial services and, indeed, of credit institutions within the Community's internal market programme.

The three chapters are closely related. The main arguments to be put forward may be summarized as follows:

1 The free market economic pattern is the workable environment aimed at by credit institutions, both at an international and European level, in order to develop their future commercial strategies.
2 The way towards 'self-regulation' lies below the recent trend on financial services 'deregulation'. Therefore the EC harmonization process has been prepared bearing in mind this final stage, despite many interests in maintaining the banking regulation '*rebus sic stantibus*'.
3 As a logical consequence of the two points above, the EC harmonization process for banking activities suffers from 'legal schizophrenia'. On the one hand, the completion of the internal market for credit institutions is not related to the legal nature of the majority of the rest of the harmonization processes. Therefore, we can say that the completion of the internal market for credit institutions is a single objective not necessarily linked to the rest of the objectives within the Commission's White Paper. On the other hand, the legal nature of the banking harmonisation process is far from clear. First, the Second Directive did not have to be enacted under articles related to freedom to provide both establishment and services. Second, we need a uniform banking law. Banking questions are too numerous and too important for all the citizens of the European Community. More than a 'technocratic' approach is necessary on the subject. A legal solution under article 235 or

220 could provide a wider range of solutions for the many problems posed by the provision of banking services across the European frontiers.

4 The above situation is the consequence of the lack of willingness of the Member States' governments to promote a European legal environment for banking services.

Two reasons seem to underly this attitude. First, there are fears of being deprived of sovereignty on monetary issues (which also means macroeconomic planing: budget, inflation, unemployment and so on) and the control of several segments of the credit market by publicly owned credit institutions. Second, there is the strong pressure on the part of the managers of the most important European credit institutions over the strategic decision-making targets.

In the following chapters we shall see how complicated the situation appears to be and how far we are from any solution involving wider citizen participation in the decision-making process on the subject. Lack of democracy and social control as regards the regulation of the activities of such a crucial sector of the economy must be regarded as basic problems to be solved in order to achieve a more reliable legislation for the regulation of financial services in Europe.

6 The Reform Proposals of the US Financial Markets

The Economic Context of Financial Services in the Near Future

It is a fact that the world's current sociopolitical environment is dominated by the most neoliberalist ideas. Economic theorists, such as Hayek[1] and Stigler,[2] form the intellectual core of the new sociopolitical environment. On the other hand, the recent political changes within the Communist bloc have contributed to the reinforcement of the economic neoliberal ideology. Therefore, the question on what industrial policy will be developed by the Western countries within the above environment ought to be answered.

The European Community, despite its peculiarities, shares the worlds' economic tendencies. Thus, beneath the majority of the Community's regulatory strategies there are economic considerations aiming to shape the sociopolitical reality in line with major Western trends.

The main purpose of these reflections is to suggest the interrelationship between the economic agents and policy-makers as regards the shaping of the economic policies to be developed by the European institutions. Pedersen is well aware of such strategy:

> It is big business which has the capacity to handle an internal EC market with all its range of regulations, complex legal systems, etc. Big business has more capacity in handling the internal market than either small and medium-sized firms or small states.[3]

The final outcome of this new economic environment raises concerns for many observers. The 'old-style' national Keynesian policy and the survival of the welfare state is as stake.[4] In many areas of Northern and Central Europe such trends will become a threat to social democratic rights as already achieved in individual Member States.

The sum of these processes is that the key relationship between the 'model' and key policy issues is the undermining of the single state as a framework for handling economic, structural, public, spatial and social dimensions. Thus, the achievement of workable markets without classical state administrative controls, and its substitution by a global market with a minimum of administrative burdens, is the goal to be achieved by these processes.

Before setting up new policy instruments and institutional arrangements in Europe, one should try to learn as much as possible from history. That is, one should evaluate different socioeconomic models and their institutional capacities to handle different kinds of problems, and avoid postulating market recommendations as the core of every economical development.

The main feature of the neoliberal tendencies is the 'self-regulatory' approach. Therefore, as we shall see in the following chapters, it is not the old trend towards deregulation as such. We shall talk of a 'new-gremialistic' approach, similar to that of the medieval commercial organization. Each of the most relevant microeconomic sectors of the economy, comprising financial services, develop a single strategy towards 'self-regulation', with its own rules, own arbitrators and so on. This complex strategy is the solution preferred by large economic organizations to the paradoxes arising from the last attempts at deregulation.

Some scholars have remarked on the attempts by economic agents to shape economic patterns in order to develop their market strategies. The majority of cited attempts were developed during the last two centuries but none of them was capable of creating a suitable economic environment. Early attempts to find solutions to both wild competence and socialism relied on 'economic protectionism' – a concept outside of the new approach.

Other historical approaches to the regulation of market structure which do not fulfil the new market regulation approach were those of Bain,[5] Waldman,[6] and Williamson,[7] as well as those of Clark, who advocated an interventionist policy constraining market power.[8]

The possibility for governments to move from 'intervention' to 'active participation' is unconvincing from the standpoint of the economic agents' interests. Such a possibility depends solely on the changing conditions of citizens' political options. Therefore, economic agents prefer to ban any possibility of government participation in the market game: no laws, no administrative agencies and so on. In effect, 'self-regulation' means absolute independence of every political decision which could hinder the aims of 'big business'. Academic support for self-regulation is easily found in the 'contestability theory' of interventionist policies, which focused increased attention upon entry barriers and redefined their character. Economies of scale, for example, have frequently been considered as barriers to entry. However, they need not permit any of the manifestations usually associated with market power. This view calls for a major reorientation of both the charters and the operating programmes of regulatory authorities.

However, the risks of a globalization of neoliberal purposes through the 'self-regulatory' approach can seriously damage the completion of the European integration objectives. The development of Western economies during the past century suggests that, with capitalism, we experience high microeconomic efficiencies, but at a price of macroeconomic inefficiencies, plus built-in socioeconomic diseconomies, large geographical inequalities and the lack of both internal and external democratic institutions to control the developmental processes. Those consequences will breach the most important aims of the citizens of Europe, expressed and consecrated through a large number of national constitutions and regulations. Moreover, these aims are expressly consecrated in both the Rome Treaty (1975) and the Single European Act (1987) and the European Union Treaty (1992).

Creating an internal market in the hope of generating market microeconomic efficiency is not very wise when one knows, from historical experience of the market system, the price in terms of social destruction. As Pedersen has warned, social destruction caused by the internal market will create a need for a mixed economy and a welfare state. As crucial dynamic processes in society generating social and economic development come from democracy at different levels, '... [a] flexible society is needed because big business will make *internal plans*. That is, we could end up in a planned economy "turned upside down"...'.[9]

The above reflections are useful in order to understand the banks' strategy at both a European and a worldwide level. Banking constitutes a microeconomic sector of the economy but, at the same time, is perhaps the most important one. As we shall see in the following chapters, the banking industry (clearly dominated by a range of no more than 100 banks in the world) is expanding its activities in many directions: securities, insurances, corporate investment and the like. Rather curiously, the above phenomena has begun to happen during the last 10 years, starting in the USA, following in Japan and, finally, in the EC.

This situation gives rise to serious concerns. Banking implies many things, including power and influence. A self-regulated banking system, with well-rooted traditions of covenants, concerted practices and oligopolistic behaviours, could constitute an independent source of power. Any relinquishment of public control over banking activities by governments or by administrative agencies may threaten the political stability of societies.

The EC internal market policy for financial services is clearly influenced by this situation, and an awareness of that fact will afford a better understanding of why the EC harmonization process is so full of contradictions, gaps and conflicting interests. Moreover, it will also lead to an understanding of the metaphoric isolation of citizens faced with the outcomes of a financial environment created for 'its own sake'.

An Historical Approach to the Reform Proposals of the US Financial Markets

On 5 February 1991, Mr Nicholas Brady presented his proposal for the 'reform' of the US financial system. The necessity to adapt the US financial markets to the development of financial products, alternative ways of resolving the inefficiencies of the deposits insurance scheme and the elimination of the restrictions imposed by the Glass-Steagall Act (1933), the Bank Holding Company Act (1956) and the McFadden Act (1927, 1933) were the main objectives to be achieved by the above 'reform'.[10]

On the table now are two more proposals for dealing with these problems: a draft approved by the House Banking Committee in June and one from the Senate Banking Committee, dated 3 August 1991. A study of these objectives can shed some light on some of the aspects underlying the EC harmonization process in financial services. In order to do so, three questions must be analysed:

1. What is the historical background of the US reform?
2. Does there exist a dichotomy between regulation versus deregulation, underlying the above 'reformist proposals'?
3. What is its relationship with the 'neoliberal' approach (through microeconomic deregulation, and the shaping macroeconomic environments)?

As regards the historical approach to the 'reform', Scholtand draws some basic features of general importance:

> We so often fail to see that the political process from which every regulatory program emerged is itself a strong kind of free market, albeit with buying power distributed differently from economic markets. The political and economic 'markets' are importantly related through such linkages as campaign financing and lobbying.[11]

The many directions towards which the 1991 'reform' of the US markets are leading are simply doors opened by the pressure of market forces over a sector of the US economy which has been highly regulated since its creation in the last century.

A comprehensive review of each of the reasons for the regulatory strategy developed in the USA is beyond the scope of this overview. However, it is worth noting the main features of some of them. The major impetus for most regulations affecting the banking industry was the stock market collapse of 1929.[12] A large body of financial reform legislation was passed in reaction to the collapse of the banking system, attempting to upgrade bank safety by limiting competition and by restricting bank entry into non-bank financial activities. Friedman and Schwartz identified the wild free play of competitive forces, which engaged banks and financial markets in unsound activities, as the major reason for the 'reform'[13] – a view which is widely shared by the majority of scholars.[14]

The most important legislative outcomes of the 1930s financial reform were the Banking Acts of 1933 and 1935. Three major provisions must be noted within the Banking Act of 1933. The first is the separation of commercial banking from investment banking, implemented by the prohibition on commercial banks from underwriting and distributing stocks, bond or other securities other than federal government bonds, municipal general obligations bonds and deposit type securities. The second is the authorization to the Federal Reserve (FED) to regulate the amount of interest that banks could pay on time deposits. The last major step in fashioning the federal bank regulatory system occurred in 1956 with the passage of the Bank Holding Company Act, which gave the FED full regulatory authority over multibank holding companies, and which was extended in 1970 to all bank holding companies whether single-bank or multi-bank. The third is the creation of the Federal Deposit Insurance Corporation (FDIC).[15]

The Banking Act of 1935 extended the power of the Federal Reserve Board by authorizing it to impose credit controls, to regulate the discount rates of the district banks and to change reserve requirements within a wide range.

The reform legislation of the 1930s determined the structure of the financial system that existed up until the passage of the Deregulation and Monetary Control Act in March 1980. Lash synthesized the process towards new financial regulation with these words:

> Because successive crisis led legislators to believe that banking required increasingly more regulation, the earlier acts were primarily designed to tighten bank regulations. In the last two decades, however, rapidly rising market interest rates, in combination with major technological innovations in communication and data processing, have caused a number of regulations to have harmful effects on depository institutions.[16]

The first legislative outcome related to these events was the Depository Institutions Deregulation and Monetary Control Act of 1980 (DIDMCA), which reduced regulation by eliminating state usury ceilings and tightened monetary control by extending FED requirements to all commercial banks.

Sharing the DIDMCA's spirit was the GARN (St Germain Depository Institutions Act of 1982) whose major purpose was to improve the situation of the 'savers' by granting them new asset and deposit powers.

In its approach towards achieving financial soundness, however, current legislation is different to that of the 1930s. The former was based in the restraining of competitive forces, whereas a sound financial system is now regarded as one in which competitive forces are allowed more flexibility.

The Need for Regulation

The 1991 proposal contains the common core of the deregulatory measures described above. After a study of each of them, we can formulate the likely patterns within which financial services are going to be developed in the future.

The majority of the measures raise the question of their necessity. In addition, it seems that only geographical constraints on bank expansion (McFadden Act, 1927; 1933) and the administrative structure of banking activities control do need to be changed. On that basis, the underlying philosophy of the remainder of the proposals must be questioned. Three of them are very important for the purposes of this research. First, a necessary consequence of the 'reform' should be the creation of a financial sector within which banks keep the pre-eminent role. Second, the elimination of restrictions from the Glass-Steagall Act (1933) and the Bank Holding Company Act (1956) will demolish the wall between the 'financial' and the 'real' economic sectors. Stock markets will be invaded by the banks' investment in securities. Finally, insurance could become another 'plus' to the banks' strategies towards the control of the financial world.

Thus, it is worth putting forward a long series of arguments from the scholars against the current tendencies towards both deregulation and self-regulation.

1 After the elimination of those forms of regulation for which there is no business support, competition would be weaker than it is now.
2 Calculations of benefits to consumers from deregulation are often based on assumptions that cannot be fully sustained. We do not know as much about the income and price elasticities of demand as we

would like. In the area of production also, our knowledge is incomplete, especially as regards economies of scale.

3 There is a potential danger to certain classes of small business if there were economies of scale.
4 There is a public distrust of the price mechanism: excessive profits from economies of scale are frequently the result not of efficiency but of market power.[17]
5 As regards social damage arising from deregulation, Redisch states that:

> The competitive process improves resource use in the long term in part by a process of social Darwinism that can destroy jobs, put firms out of business, or both.[18] White shares this view as regards large firms driving out the small firms, stating that at the end of this process, monopoly–oligopoly will prevail in the market with 'the likely abuses of monopoly–oligopoly'.[19]

6 Political power will increase as a result of the increasing aggregate concentration of bank holding company acquisitions.[20]
7 Distorting managerial effects (conflict of interest) is another risk associated with permitting banks to engage in investment banking, or to offer commingled investment funds.[21] Here, Opper has strongly criticized three consequences of the banks' participation in the business that traditionally had belonged to the securities industry:

   a as regards the bank's role as both investment banker and potential lender to the same issues;
   b as regards the impact of the investment banking business on the overall riskiness of the bank;
   c as regards the competitive effect of banks' investment banking activities on the securities industry.[22]

8 Savage and Solomon are of the opinion that the branching gains to competition, deriving from deregulation, are only temporary. The larger banks, through their branches, will soon drive all of the smaller banks out of existence, leaving the industry to the oligopolistic practices of a few giants.[23]
9 Variable-rate premium insurance schemes would involve a higher average premium than the present system.[24]
10 There is a possibility that existing firms would try to protect their market shares by setting an entry-forestalling price. Such a practice

will make it unprofitable for new firms to enter and will thus maintain the monopoly positions of existing banks.[25]

11 There is no evidence that deregulation will benefit consumers, as regards the level of saving rates actually paid, due to the higher degree of concentration.[26]

12 Baldwin and McCrudden have discovered some negative aspects of the 'deregulation–self-regulation' proposals:

   a Basic democratic principles could be damaged, as previously noted by the Wilson Committee, following the Radcliffe Committee before it.
   b controls in the field of investor protection might also be damaged in a 'self-regulatory' environment.
   c The kinds of decision made in gaming regulation could not be wholly consistent with the supply of full information to applicants.
   d The problem of assessing effective enforcement in the context of agency action is also at stake.[27]

Consequently, we must be sceptical about substituting regulation by market discipline in the control of risk-taking by banking firms in 'today's aggressive, trading oriented banking environment'.[28] As regards proposals relying on the viability of private, large-scale deposit insurance, the risk of contagious runs and macroeconomic disturbances (monetary shocks, velocity shocks, price-level shocks, and the difficulty of determining which insolvent banks should be closed or reorganized) are problems that a private agency could not easily solve.[29]

All the features described above pave the way to several hypotheses. First, are the managers of the most important US credit institutions aiming to dismantle every regulatory organization within which politics could influence their business strategies? (Note that the agencies depending on the US administration are being run by experts which, at least apparently, are free of business control.) Second, do they pretend to create new agencies under the control of experts linked directly or indirectly to the credit institutions? Third, is there any possibility of 'exporting' the new financial regulatory environment to both the European and the Japanese markets?

Notes

1 F. Hayek, *New Studies in Philosophy, Politics, Economics and the History of Ideas*, London, 1978.
2 G. Stigler, *The Citizen and the State*, Chicago, 1975.

3 J.S. Pedersen, *A Multi-dimensional Analysis of Aspects of Economic and Monetary Union in the European Community* (a commentary), EUI, 1990, p. 7.
4 Ibid., p. 8.
5 J.S. Bain, *Barriers to New Competition*, 1951.
6 D.E. Waldman, *Antitrust Action and Market Structure*, 1978.
7 O.F. Williamson, *Markets and Hierarchies. Analysis and Antitrust Implications*, 1975, pp. 111–13.
8 J.B. Clark, '*The Control of Trust*', *An Argument in Favour of Curbing the Power of Monopoly by a Natural Method*, 1987.
9 J.S. Pedersen, op. cit., p. 11.
10 See ICE, *Boletín Económico*, Ministerio de Economía y Hacienda, no. 2272, 18–24 March 1991, pp. 863 et seq.
11 R.A. Schotland, 'An Overview: New Myths and Old Realities' in *The Deregulation of the Banking and Securities Industries*, Lexington Books, 1979, p. 20.
12 N.A. Lash, *Banking Laws and Regulations*, New Jersey: Prentice-Hall, 1987, p. 12.
13 M. Friedman and A.J. Schwartz, *A Monetary History of the United States: 1867–1960*, Princeton University Press, 1967, pp. 311–12.
14 T.H.F. Cargill and G.G. Garcia, *Financial Deregulation and Monetary Control*, Stanford University Press, 1982, p. 9.
15 The FDIC insures bank deposits up to some maximum, $2500 at its inception, and is funded by a flat charge of one-twelfth of one per cent of total domestic deposits.
16 N.A. Lash, *Banking Laws* ..., op. cit., p. 20.
17 M. Hou-Thakker, 'Economic Aspects of Deregulation' in *Deregulating American Industry*, Lexington Books 1977, pp. 5 et seq.
18 N.A. Redisch, in Pedersen, op. cit., note 9.
19 L.J. White, in Pedersen, op. cit., note 9, p. 109.
20 On analysing the evolution of cited developments within the USA, they fear that the USA would be dominated by large financial and industrial conglomerates similar to the Zaibatsu (Japan). See R.J. Lawrence and S.M. Talley, 'An Assessment of Bank Holding Companies', *Federal Reserve Bulletin*, January 1976, p. 20.
21 F.R. Edwards, 'Banks and Securities Activities: Legal and Economic Perspectives on the Glass-Steagall Act' in R.A. Schotland, *The Deregulation* ...' op. cit., p. 280 et seq.
22 F.P. Opper, 'Comment' to the 'Deregulation of the Intersection' in R.A. Schotland, *The Deregulation* ...' op. cit., pp. 347–8.
23 D.T. Savage, and E.H. Solomon, 'Bank Branching: the Competitive Issues', *Journal of Bank Research*, Summer 1980.
24 Barnett, Horvitz and Silverberg, 'Deposit Insurance: the Present System and Some Alternatives, *Banking Law Journal*, April 1977.
25 J.S. Bain, *Barriers to New Competition*, Cambridge Mass.: Harvard University Press, 1956.
26 Ware, 'Banking Structure and Performance', *Federal Reserve Bank of Cleveland Economic Review*, March 1972, p. 3–14. See also Vernon, 'Separation of Ownership and Control and Profit Rates: the Evidence from banking Comment', *Quarterly Journal of Financial and Quantitative Analysis* (1), January 1971, pp. 615–25.
27 R. Baldwin and C.H. McCrudden, *Regulation and Public Law*, London: Weidenfeld and Nicholson, 1987, pp. 300–30.
28 W.S. Haraf, 'Toward a Sound Financial System' in M. Friedman and A.J. Schwartz, *Financial Deregulation* ..., op. cit., p. 181.
29 Ibid., pp. 182–5.

7 The Importance of the Euromarket

The aim of this chapter is to analyse some of the aspects underlying the EC approach to the banking harmonization process. Three major features of the study can be noted: first, similarities can be established between the US and the European credit institutions' attitude towards regulation – namely in their strategies for the achievement of a 'deregulated' environment within which they can develop their market policies and profit from freedom in the widest possible sense. Thus, the self-regulation trend can also be found discerned underlying the aims of the European credit institutions.

Second, the above situation influences the shaping of the institutional framework, currently under discussion, for the regulation of the European financial markets, principally with regard to the competencies to be given to the administrative agencies for the control of the credit institutions' behaviour in the market. The lack of a well-defined plan for the creation of a European Central Bank is one of its consequences.

Third, any study of the Euromarket will demonstrate its importance as another root factor of the EC banking harmonization process. The aim of this analysis is to show the importance of achieving 'deregulatory' framework in order to prevent money, which is currently placed in accounts in settled European countries, flowing out to offshore banks.

Several Factors Underlying the EC Banking Harmonization Process in Financial Services

A long list of arguments, slightly different from those given by the Commission for the completion of the internal market for financial services,[1] seem to underlie the banking harmonization process in the EC. Cited arguments refer to different aspects: market, developments, international pressures, credit institutions' strategies and so on, and are listed below.

1 The lack of identity of European banking landscape.[2] A resemblance to the US future banking landscape can be found in many aspects: the existence of a small number of large banks controlling wide segments of the market, the achievement of economies of scale, the credit institutions' plans to develop future expansion strategies in terms of cross-shareholdings and affiliations rather than by major takeovers and so on.
2 The significant role of 'External interests' in the achievement of an integrated financial market.[3]
3 The creation, by Credit institutions, of holding companies with portfolios covering different industries.[4]
4 The importance of increased competition which is driving banks towards offering non-bank services; the nature of the interaction of the globalized financial markets (and the efforts to face up to it, notably through the proposals of the Cook Committee) and the EC's Second Banking Directive; the role played by financial institutions in mergers and acquisitions, and so on.
5 'Despecialization' (the recent tendency to merge banking and insurance activities), as well as 'disintermediation' on securities markets, (increased capital requirements and the greater need for risk management induce banks to make their assets increasingly secure), which are factors moving credit institutions to achieve wider margins of competence within the highly regulated European market.[6]
6 The influence exercised by international banks within the Basle Committee, as a very important initial step towards the harmonization process in Europe.[7]
7 As regards the shaping of the future institutional pattern for the regulation of the European financial market, the theories of Tobin[8] and Goodfriend-King,[9] which rely exclusively on the lender of last resort intervention, seem to form the philosophy underlying the European Commission proposals, although they are not specifically mentioned. Here, the influence of current US deregulatory strategies, supported by the best-positioned European credit institutions, can be clearly seen.
8 The neccessity to adapt the existing European regulatory structures with a view to integrating national financial systems in a coherent framework, resulting from the synergic interactions of several international factors.[10] These include the linkage of the various markets through both securitization and financial innovation (for instance, index futures, options and swaps) which will lead towards a 'requalification' of banking strategies in the retail market.[11] Therefore, current EC regulatory strategies, based on 'minimal harmonization', will permit a much

more sophisticated use of financial and credit investments leading to a replacement of individual saving by collective management of loanable funds. 'Second-class' savers do not seem to gain much benefit from the harmonization process.[12]

9 According to Steinherr, even if there were no widespread cross-border establishment of banks, the structure of the banking industry in Europe would change dramatically.[13] Therefore any attempt to look for a clear, independent European strategy on the subject seems to meet with little success.

10 Importance must be given to the agenda of the Uruguay Round negotiations within the GATT, which, for the first time, included talks designed to liberalize international financial services. The common core of discussions within the Financial Services Group (including the USA, the EC and the developing countries largest credit institutions) were arguments for 'cross-sectoral linkage'.[14]

11 Agreements on capital adequacy between the Member states signatories of the Bank for International Settlements (BIS), in order to withstand the increasing fragility of international capital markets, must also be considered as another factor influencing the EC harmonization process.[15]

12 The importance of filling gaps in the international accountability rules in order to deal with the existence of new financial instruments, (for example, SWAP, FRA, CAP, FLOOR, COLLAR, NIF, RUF).[16] This view echoes that of Marsh about the necessity of avoiding a crash of the fragile international capital markets.[17]

13 Tax fluctuations within the banking loan markets, risks arising from interest rates, position risks, and such like. Due to their international nature, all these problems have to be solved within a global market approach; thereby leaving no scope for single European strategies on the subject.

14 Carr maintains that the original driving forces of change can be found in the deregulation of the European securities business, the rise of the Euromarkets, and the supersedence of the international capital and currency market over domestic ones. Their impact on bank business has been amplified by the computer and telecommunications revolution. Therefore, the move towards a larger and more unified financial services market in Europe was under way long before the European Commission thought it was a good idea. Moreover, the imposition of the Basle Committee rules governing capital adequacy, and their efforts to standardize bank business and accounting practices, will present more of a headache than a heart attack for the big banks. Indeed, most

of them already conform to such rules.[19] In fact, only some of the anti-competitive aspects of structural regulation have been relaxed.[20]

15 Both the neoliberal economic climate of the 1980s and the influence on the European market of world market developments have played a decisive role.[21] The European decision-makers' lack of autonomy on financial issues is one of the most relevant features of the harmonization process: 'Expansionary' (contradictionary) policies will be offset by capital outflows (inflows), particularly when domestic and foreign interest-bearing assets are close substitutes and will thus no longer be able to exert a (negative) demand stimulus on the 'real' economy.[22]

16 The main reason for regulation in banking is not for the protection of depositors but for the stability of banking markets in Europe.[23]

17 We can identify two forces that led to the decline of current European regulation in banking: technology and the inefficiency of the arbitrary segmentation of financial product lines across industries. To the extent that these forces are truly universal, the study of the European harmonization process can be focused on different root factors than those of the Commission proposals.[24]

Thus, it may be suggested that a sort of fundamental harmonization – concerning principles if not details – has been pressed upon the European 'regulators' by the events outlined above, rather than by any 'specific' EC plan aiming at a rational harmonization in this field.

Several conclusions can be drawn from the above analysis. First, external markets are exerting pressure in order to relax the European financial markets to allow the development of third country credit institutions strategies. Most of the features noted above are related to the completion of a worldwide financial market, within which only big banks could play. Therefore the Cecchini promises, mainly regarding advantages for consumers so far as retail banking is concerned, are far from being achieved by the harmonization process. In this sense, a recent study by Simon Brady[25] shows that banks were well aware that benefits would not come from interpenetration into competitors' retail banking markets; profits from international operations remain small in stark contrast to the losses they can incur.[26] Similarly, a Salomon Brothers report notes that:

> The most important deregulation is that which is bringing down the barriers within countries, not that which in theory allows cross-border competition.[27]

Second, the 'despecialization trend' accompanies the toppling of regulatory barriers. The forces driving banks into insurance are complex. Separation between the two industries was imposed by regulatory restraints which are now being dismantled. Long-term strategists talk of the struggle for savings in an increasingly competitive market. Therefore, banks must struggle to defend their market share of savings against the life insurance and pensions industry, and against various forms of collective investments vehicles such as unit trusts.[28]

Third, the role played by international agencies and organizations, within which lobby the largest banks in the world, has been very important in the shaping of the banking harmonization process in Europe. GATT negotiations, the Cook Committee recommendations through the BIS Basle agreements, and OECD strategies underlie the EC rules on the subject.

Fourth, both financial innovations and technological developments pave the way to the globalization of financial markets. The EC harmonization process takes good account of that situation.

The Influence of Current Deregulatory Strategies on the Shaping of the EC Central Bank

The new emphasis on market forces, the lower estimate of the value of government intervention and public expenditure, and the vogue for deregulation have, at one and the same time, undermined the plausibility of a Central Bank conception linked to a 'public policy' strategy. The increasing globalization of banking activities, and the largest world credit institutions' strategies for the near future, provoked the emergence of lobby relationships between credit institutions and public authorities. Therefore, the existence of the Central Bank, and the process being developed, and to be developed, before its creation should be questioned. Should the Bank function as Cantillon's eighteenth-century ideas proposed? That is, to be merely the creator of money, and a supervisor of its fluctuations, without any other regulatory or sanctionary power. Should it display a 'lender of last resort' policy? Should it be vested with the whole range of powers currently exercised by most of the Central Banks of the EC countries? Whatever the answer should be, it is clear from the historical evolution towards Economic and Monetary Union within the EC that the idea of creating a Central Bank for Europe was always present, but that only recently have serious steps towards its creation been taken, up to the point of its inclusion in the Economic and Monetary Union Treaty.

Barre's report in the late 1960s,[29] as well as the 1970 'Commission memorandum' on the monetary union,[30] set monetary mechanisms at a European level to resemble those used by Central Banks at national level. The Werner report[31] a product of the European Council of the Hague,[32] called for the financial integration in European banking systems, as well as for the achievement of economic and monetary integration in Europe through the transfer of competencies to the European institutions. The Werner report (the basis of the Council Resolution of 22 March 1971)[33] did not specify the terms of nor the conditions governing a European Central Bank. Nor did the Commission Report of 30 April 1973[34] help to clarify the issue.

We could explain the silence of the European institutions in two ways. First, the governments of the Community Member States were not too faithful to the achievement of European Economic and Monetary Union. Thus, the formation of a European Central Bank made no sense. This idea can be sustained if we understand the various reports as a 'psychological reaction' to the crisis provoked by M. De Gaulle in 1965, The Empty Chair Policy. Taking into account that The Hague summit was held a few months after the political demise of De Gaulle, the aim of giving an impression of the European project's unity and efficiency to European citizens could be a valid reason. Second, the 'international context of *Pax Bancaria'* could prevent any temptation on the part of banking organizations to lobby the European institutions.

Whatever the reason, the fact is that it was not until 1977 that the European institutions came to a political compromise on the achievement of an Economic and Monetary Union. The Jenkins lecture at the European University Institute,[35] which demanded wider margins of competencies for the European institutions, was the cornerstone of a long series of debates within the European Council: Copenhagen,[36] Bremen[37] and Brussels.[38] It was the Council Resolution of the former which constituted the legal point of reference for the existence of article 102-A of the Single European Act, in which the possibility for an institutional reform of the Treaties on monetary issues was stated. Despite the complexity of the procedure set out by article 102-A as regards procedures to be enacted for the reform of the Treaty, the first steps towards the creation of a European Central Bank have been taken alongside the institutional proposals.

On the other hand, several well known European politicians have stressed the necessity of creating a European Central Bank: Spinelli,[39] Thorn,[40] and Gonzalez,[41] among others made a political compromise by accepting the creation of a European Central Bank as an unconditional link to the achievement of European Monetary Union. In this sense, a passing mention should be made of the 'draft' adopted by the European Parliament on 14 February 1984 on 'The European Union Treaty', of which article 51, entitled 'Credit Policy', says:

> The Union shall exercise concurrent competence as regards European monetary and credit policies, with the particular objective of coordinating the use of capital market resources by the creation of a European capital market committee and the establishment of a European bank supervisory authority.[42]

However, the most important step was the Delors' *Report on Economic and Monetary Union in the European Community.*[43] Point 19 of section 1, chapter II of the Report says:

> A monetary union would require a single monetary policy and responsibility for the formulation of this policy would consequently have to be vested in one decision making body.

This idea was stressed by point 24 of section 2, chapter II:

> The responsibility for the single monetary policy would have to be vested in a new institution, in which centralized and collective decisions would be taken on the supply of money and credit as well as on other instruments of monetary policy, including interest rates.

After describing some of the competencies of the new monetary institution to be created in the final stage of Economic and Monetary Union, point 31 of section 4, chapter II places the new institutions 'within the constellation of Community Institutions', which means at the same level as that the European Council, European Parliament, Council of Ministers, the EC Commission and the European Court of Justice. Therefore, will it not have the range of an 'ancillary institution'?

Point 32 of section 32, chapter II, specified both the name of the most remarkable features of the new institution:

> Considering ... the domestic and international monetary policy making of the Community should be organized in a federal form, in what might be called a European System of Central Banks (ESCB) .... An autonomous Community institution ... consists of a central institution (with its own balance sheet) and the national central banks.

The system is entrusted to regulate price stability, monetary policy, exchange rate, reserve management, payment system and the coordination of banking supervision policies of the supervisory authorities, active within a *federative structure.*

The European Councils of Madrid,[44] Strasbourg,[45] Dublin,[46] and Rome ('ad hoc')[47] gave political support to the content of the Delors' Report, which is substantially reproduced in articles 104, 104A-B, 105, 106, 107, 108 and 109 of the Economic and Monetary Union Treaty (Maastricht, 1991).

Despite the progress which has been made, two important issues must be resolved: the extent of the transfer of budgetary powers to Community level, and the content of the intermediate stages before full powers are transferred to the Central Bank.

The solution of those questions is directly linked to the future strategies to be developed by credit institutions. A substantial number of competencies transferring, in the near future, to the European System of Central Banks will ensure that the European Central Banks authorities will become the new focal point for lobbying.

We can therefore talk of a 'second best' when referring to the interest for banks' strategies in the creation of a European Central Bank. Current lobbying is being performed on two levels: the national and that of the European institutions. The transfer of competencies to a single European institution will necessarily increase the effectiveness of bank lobbying. In this sense, it is worthwhile drawing some conclusions:

1 The rapid developments in recent years towards the achievement of an Economic and a Monetary Union coincide with the worldwide trend towards the globalization of financial services, described earlier. Analysis of the historical evolution of the European Economic and Monetary Union has shown that nothing of importance was done before 1986. The agreement reached at Apeldoorn by the Ministries of Economy and Finance of the EEC[48] paved the way for the signing of the Economic and Monetary Union Treaty in Maastricht. Therefore, it must be questioned what, if any, are the forces supporting these changes: a political will of European integration? macroeconomic strategies for the consolidation of the Single Market? decisions reached at a supra communitarial level (G-10, OECD, G-7...) within which the world's largest financial services institutions are especially powerful?
2 Although, to date, the features of the future Central Bank have not been wholly shaped, the current pattern of the Bundesbank seems to be the desired model. Therefore, as the Bundesbank is credited with full credibility as an inflation-averse Central Bank, the future Central Bank will develop conservative policies.[49] As most scholars seem to consider that this credibility is largely due to the 'formal independence' of the Bundesbank,[50] – a status expected by the European Central Banking System vis-à-vis both national governments and EC institutions – it is not too difficult to believe that bankers will be satisfied with its creation. This view is emphasized by the fact that the legitimate concern of all Central Banks – not only the Bundesbank – is to assure to the monetary authorities, called upon to manage a Federal European Bank, a sufficient degree of independence vis-à-vis political authorities, which are always suspected of inflationary laxity regarding the financing of internal deficits through money creation. Therefore, if the appointment of the Board

of Governors of the European Central Bank were left exclusively to the governors of the national Central Banks, despite the fact that these would obviously consult first with their Ministers of Finance, they would be far less dependent on national political authorities than most Central Bank governors are today.

As was stated before, the enactment of anti-inflationary measures[51] and independence are the most identifiable features of the banking strategies influencing the decision-making processes of Western societies. Moreover, taking into account that the concept of universal banking is most clearly found in the German regulation of its financial markets, the creation of a European Central Bank will undoubtedly guarantee the continuity of worldwide current tendencies towards universal banking.

3 The centralization trend seems to be pointing towards making the European Central Bank the eventual 'single banking agency'. If the regulatory balance moves in the near future from the government towards the market, the creation of a European Central Bank could seriously damage the current imbalance of economic and monetary powers between government and business managers, particularly if, as some European countries have proposed (for example, the UK and Holland), the self-regulation trend shapes the creation of the European Central Bank. A board of governors constituted by 'independent specialists' coming from private business, and vested with a small number of competencies (similar to those developing by a lender of last resort), will be an easy target for manipulation by private interests.

These hypotheses find theoretical support among the strong criticisms from the winner of the Nobel Prize in economics, Maurice Allais, regarding the current conditions underlying the creation of a European Central Bank.[52] The issues at stake are the democratic control and the kind of monetary policy the Community might pursue through its own Central Bank. A Central Bank restricted to acting to counter inflation and ensuring monetary stability, while the key decisions affecting growth, employment and living standards are essentially taken by free-market forces, could not be used as a positive instrument of public policy to achieve aims which include the optimization of growth. It is much more than a purely technical monetary or financial question. A lack of democratic control on the subject could endanger the economic goals laid down by the Community's democratic decision-making institutions. If the system is to survive, we need a political will to proceed along this path, or, in the longer run, the completion of the internal market will generate forces which will threaten the achievement of economic efficiency within the EC.[53]

The above arguments are reinforced by the fact that the new supranational financial markets need some kind of supranational surveillance, equivalent of a Central Bank or supervisory authority. Therefore it is not difficult to imagine that this newly created supranational institution will be vested with a minimum of competencies, principally because the possibility of the creators of this supranational market reaching an agreement as regards the allocation of a large range of competencies within the supranational institution is far from certain. On the contrary, the creation of the said institution should be regarded from the perspective of a 'lender of last resort' whose competencies shall be limited to assessing risk and devising appropriate prudential safeguards. This solution will be in line with current regulatory approaches adopted by Western policy-makers, mainly because it is easier to reach a common agreement to pass from 'current cooperation' between monetary authorities to 'common participation' in a supranational institution vested with a limited number of competencies.[54]

The Importance of the Euromarket in the Shaping of the EC Current Financial Services Regulatory Strategies

The growth of the Eurocurrency deposit market,[55] which has been stimulated by the exemption of Eurocurrency deposits from monetary controls in the form of minimum reserve requirements,[56] raises the awkward question of what will happen after 1992 to that part of it which is placed in accounts based on EC territory.[57] The Commission's proposals for the achievement of an integrated financial market, though not including any specific mention of the above question, have considered its existence. Principally, we notice that this supranational market magnifies every problem of complexity posed by the regulation of domestic banking. Therefore it is useful both to give a historical perspective of the development of this market and to show why it is important for European regulators (and, indeed, for European credit institutions) to retain control over its future development.

The Euromarket developed on its own. It just corresponded to a need and was the result of excessive regulations in other markets. The Euromarket was absolutely necessary, not just in financial services, not just in services in general but also for industry. In this sense it is worth mentioning some of the factors contributing to both its creation and growth.[58] The first factor was the use, by UK merchant banks, of the US dollar for external loans from accounts based in London, in the late 1950s.[59]

The second factor was the birth of 'international banking',[60] as a consequence of the monetary restrictions mainly imposed by Regulation Q and the Interest Equalization Tax in the USA.[61]

The third factor was the economic 'shock' provoked by the 1970s' oil crisis. Since the great rise in oil prices at the end of 1973 the markets have been important in recycling the deposits of oil-rich states, especially to poor countries: between 1973 and the end of the decade Euromarket lending to non-oil exporting, less developed countries rose nearly ninefold, to account for over 40 per cent of all loans.[62]

Another factor was the suspension of dollar convertibility[63] and, finally, the Russians' deposits in European dollars accounts (instead of US-based accounts, because of the 'Cold War') needed for international trade transactions.[64]

In the mid-1970s the amount of currencies 'floating' within the Euromarket was, in the opinion of London, one of the reasons for the conclusion of both the 1975 and the 1983 Basle agreements.[65] Since the Euromarket stood as entity in its own right, the monetary authorities of the Group of Ten decided to formulate some minimum rules for its functioning. This policy making was strengthened after the 1974 Herstatt and the 1977 Banco Ambrosiano scandals. In fact, the influence of the 1983 Basle agreement was discernible in the 1983 and the 1986 EEC Banking Directives, regarding the supervision of the credit institutions on a consolidated basis and the annual accounts respectively. The former of the above Directives was an attempt by the European regulators to establish minimum standards to the development of new financial instruments within the Euromarket.

Those attempts, though regrettable from a 'prudential' perspective, did not create a regulatory framework capable of guaranteeing the stability of the Euromarket.

Those features above provide us with some foundations to show the connection between the minimalist approach of the Commission's proposals for the creation of a unified financial market in Europe and the Euromarket itself:

1 The EC has sufficient self-interest to allow 'certain islands' to remain within the Community. The special status of the Euromarket[66] will provide European companies with both extensive and flexible financing.
2 The fact that non-EC centres (for example, Singapore and Hong Kong) have not taken over the Eurodollar market suggests that, if the EC re-regulates, the Eurodollar market is likely to migrate to non-EEC countries.[67] Therefore, only a de-regulatory strategy could help to maintain EC-based Eurodollar accounts in Europe.

Both the governments of the EC Member States and the European credit institutions are well aware of this situation. Due to the fact that Eurocurrency operations occur 'offshore', but not beyond the reach of governments, Eurocurrency banks could be regulated on a territorial basis. The political and economic implications of this situation are important. Thus, the net regulatory burden of the EC must be commensurate with that in other industrial countries. If not, there will be a migration of financial services to third countries.

The question still remains of how much of the Euromarkets profit adversely affect European welfare standards. What is clear is that it is vitally important for the European banks' day-to-day financial strategies to keep control over one of the world's most deregulated financial markets.

Notes

1 See Chapter 8.
2 S. Bellanger, 'Toward an Integrated European Banking System: 1992 and Beyond', *The Bankers Magazine*, **171** (4), July–August, 1988.
3 S. Carletti and S. Aaronson, 'Which Banks can Bank on 1992?' in I. Gillespie (ed.), *Banking 1992. A Eurostudy Special Report*, 1991. pp. 55–80.
4 '...the holding companies that seem likely to arise in many cases will probably include a bank or a financial services company of some sort ...'. (The recent siege laid by De Benedetti and the Compagnie Financière de Mez against Societé Générale de Belgique can provide us a good example.) See, J. Revell, 'Bank Preparations for 1992: Some Clues and Some Queries', *Revue de la Banque. Bank en Financiewezen*, March 1989.
5 See N. Thygesen, 'Introduction' to *Financial Institutions in Europe Under New Competitive Conditions*, Dordrecht: Kluwer Academic Publishers, 1990, pp. 3–7.
6 A. Steinherr and C. Gilibert, 'The impact of Financial Market Integration on the European Banking Industry', *CEPS* (1), 1989.
7 P.A.M. Cornet, 'Issues in Banking Supervision and Regulation from the Perspective of a Banking Supervisor', in N. Thygesen, *Financial Institutions ...*'; op. cit., p. 279.
8 J. Tobin, 'The Case for Preserving Regulatory Distinctions' in *Restructuring the Financial System. Symposium of the FRB*, Kansas City, 1987.
9 Goodfriend-King, *Financial Deregulation, Monetary Policy and Central Banking*, Rochester, 1987.
10 Dini notes some factors: (a) the uncertain economic environment of the past two decades with high volatility of inflation, interest rates, exchange rates and umprecedented inbalances in current accounts; (b) rapid technical progress in data processing and telecommunications; (c) greater reliance on the allocative efficiency of a properly functioning price system. See L. Dini, 'Financial Markets Revolution: International Diagnosis and Implications for the Banking Sector', Communication to the 20th Congress of the CICP, Marrakech, 20 October, 1988.
11 G. Visentini, 'Le recenti evoluzioni nella disciplina dell attività finanziarie', Luiss: Appunti (1988).
12 C.H. Croisset, 'Si les banques venaient à disparaître quelles seraient les raisons de les réinventer?' in *La Revue Banque* (490), January 1989.
13 See A. Steinherr, 'Integrated Financial Market' in *European Affairs*, Elsevier, 1989: pp. 61, et seq.

14 See M. Westlake, 'Towards a New Financial Order', *Euromoney*, November 1990, pp. 74–8.
15 See J. Lewis and C.H. March, 'Too Many Hungry Mouths to Feed' in *Euromoney*, December 1990, pp. 33–9. See also L. Bryan, interviewed by C. Marsh, in 'The Real Issues Behind Bank Reform', *Euromoney*, March 1991, p. 34.
16 J.L. Cea Garcia, 'Los nuevos instrumentos financieros y la gestión moderna', *El País*, 27 January 1990, p. 54.
17 Mostly in countries as Italy, France, Spain and West Germany. See P. Molyneux, 'An Analysis of the Structure and Performance Characteristics of Top EC Banks and the Strategic Implications for 1992' in *Revue de la Banque* (6), June 1989, pp. 359–66.
18 P.L. Fabrizi, A. Ferrari and Erzegovesi, 'La gestione dei flussi finanziari nelle aziende di credito', *ATIC*, Milan: Guiffrè, 1990. See also E. Hoffmeyer, 'Is There Over-optimism on European Financial Integration?', *Danmarks Nationalbank Monetary Review*, February 1989, pp. 19–24.
19 J. Carr, 'Banking in Europe: a Brave New World?', *Financial Law Review*, September 1989, pp. 4–8.
20 J. Mitchell, 'Liberalisation and Regulatory reform in the Field of Banking Services in Europe', in *Liberalization and Regulatory Reform in the Field of Banking Services in Europe*, Zurich: Schulthers Polygraphischer Verlag, 1989.
21 M. Vanheukelen and J. Peckhans, *The European Integration of Financial Markets*, Maastricht: European Institute of Public Administration, 1986.
22 Ibid., p. 3.
23 E. Baltensperger and J. Dermine, 'Banking Deregulation in Europe', *Economic Policy*, **4**, 1987, pp. 63–109.
24 See A. Santomero, *et al.*, in *Bank Merger Premiums, Analysis and Evidence*, New York: Salomon Brothers, 1987. See also R. Gut, 'Financial Services, 1992 and Beyond', *Restructuring Europe's Financial Services*, Rooster, 1989, pp. 93–101.
25 See *Euromoney*, Special Supplement: *Agenda for the New Europe*, March 1991, pp. 1–22.
26 For example, Britain's National Westminster Bank: in 1989, its UK operations generated £951 million of its profits, while international operations generated just 161 million. Barclays Bank: domestic operations £1030 million; foreign operations lost over £700. Société Générale's revenues: just 14%. Deutsche Bank's: 19%; ABN/AMRO: 26%.
27 *European Banking Integration in 1992*, 1989.
28 All factors cited include potential for growth stemming from the increasing age profile of the European population and its propensity to save for retirement.
The statistical data speaks for itself: Lloyds extracts more profit from insurance business (Lloyds Abbey life: £319 million), than it does from core UK retail banking operations (£168 million). Barclays: £181 million. National Westminster: £97 million. Midland: £151 million. (All of them pre-tax.)
29 See R. Cantillon, 'Ensayo sobre la naturaleza del comercio en general', Study from Mendez Ibisate, F. in *España Economica,* February, 1990.
30 Suppl. Bull. des CE no. 3, 1969. Suppl. Bull. des CE no. 3. 1970.
31 OJ, EC, no. C, 136 of. 11-111-1970, p. 1.
32 Point 8, of the EC Council Communication of the Hague, December 1969.
33 OJ, EC, no. C, 28 of 27–3–1971, p. 1.
34 Supp. Bull. des CE, no. 5, 1973.
35 1st Jean Monnet Conference, 'L'Europe: défis actuels et perspectives d'avenir', Florence, 27 October 1977.

36 April 1978.
37 June 1978.
38 December 1978.
39 M.A. Spinelli, '*Vers L'Union Européenne*', 6th Jean Monnet Conference, Florence: EUI, June 1983.
40 G. Thorn, *Unione Europea o Declino: essere o non essere*, 7th Jean Monnet Conference, Florence: EUI, 24 May 1984.
41 F. Gonzalez Marquez, *Europa, dalla Comunità dei dodici all 'unione Europea: obiettivo 1992*, 10th Jean Monnet Conference, Florence: EUI, 19 October 1987.
42 See J. Capotorti, *The European Union Treaty*, Oxford, 1986, pp. 206–207.
43 European Council, Hanover, 27–28 June 1988.
44 26–27 June 1989.
45 December 1989.
46 25–26 June 1990.
47 27–28 October 1990.
48 21–22 September 1991.
49 See K. Rogoff, 'The Optimal Degree of Commitment to an Intermediate Target', *Quarterly Journal of Economics*, **4**, 1985, pp. 69–89.
50 See K. Russo, and G. Tullio, 'Monetary Policy Coordination within the European Monetary System: Is There a Rule?' in F. Giavazzi, S. Micossi and M. Miller (eds), *The European Monetary System*, Cambridge: Cambridge University Press, 1988. See also A. Lesina, 'Politics and Business Cycles in Industrial Democracies', *Economic Policy*, 1991.
51 See the influence of banking pressures on the Western countries' economic strategies in the chapter related to 'interests'.
52 M. Allais, Interview in *El País*, 21 July 1991.
53 The 1988 Catherwood Report estimated that the gains from the establishment of monetary union would be at least 30 billion Ecus per year. See F. McDonald and G. Zis, 'The European Monetary System: Towards 1992 and Beyond', *Journal of Common Market Studies*, **28** (3), March 1989. See also interview with Mr Lane Kirkland, *Le Figaro*, 18 September 1991, p. 11.
54 Recently, Mr Helmut Schlesinger, President of the German Bundesbank has defended the creation of a European Central Bank whose members should not be appointed by the governments of the EC Member States, and who should not themselves be politicians. See 'Economia' in *El País*, 16 November 1991, p. 38.
55 From essentially zero in 1960 to over $4.5 trillion on a gross basis and $2.2 trillion on a net basis in March 1988. (Source: Morgan Guaranty Trust; 'World Financial Markets', *Economic Report of the President*, 1989, table B-67.
56 See R.S. Dale, 'Prudential Regulation of Multinational Banking', *National Westminster Bank Quarterly Review*, February, 1981, pp. 14–24.
57 See R. Gut, Financial Services ..., op. cit., p. 96.
58 See Cohen, *Organising the World's Money: the Political Economy of International Monetary Relations*, London: 1978.
59 See Sarcinelli, 'Assetti monetari internazionali movimenti di capitali, controlli amminsitratiovi: un difficile cammino verso la libertà' in *Bancaria*, 1981, pp. 874 et seq. See also A. Dondellinger, 'Rôle et place des éstablissements financiers européens dans les marchés internationaux' in Proceedings of the *1986 Symposium on Europe and the Future* of *Financial Services*, op. cit., pp. 164 et seq.
60 See M. Lo Cicero, *L'attuazioni delle Direttive CEE in materia creditizia,* Milan: Giuffrè Editore, 1983, pp. 469 et seq.

61 See De Cecco, 'Origins of Post-war Payments System' in *Cambridge Journal of Economics*, 1979, pp. 3 et seq. See also D'Onorio 'Il governo della valuta tra souranità e interdipendenza' in *Banca, Borsa*; **1**, 1979, pp. 33 et seq.

62 See T. Killick, 'Euromarket Recycling of OPEC Surpluses', *The Banker*, January 1981, pp. 15–23.

63 See Sarcinecci, 'Nuove sfide agli euromercati e presenza delle banche italiane nella city: riflessi pre l'equilibrio esterno dell 'economia italiana' in *Bancaria*, 1980, pp. 795 et seq.

64 See Chown-Kelen, *Off-shore Investment Centres*, London, 1979.

65 See C. London, 'Le secteur bancaire du regard du droit communautaire', in *Rev. Trim. dr. Europ.*, **23** (4), October–December 1987, pp. 593 et seq.

66 Namely self-regulation exemption from the rules on publishing a prospectus for bond issues and from withholding tax.

67 See R.M. Levich, 'The Euromarkets after 1992', in J. Dermine (ed.), *European Banking in the 1990's*, 1990.

8 An Assessment of the Influence of the Globalization of the Financial Markets

The aim of this chapter is to give an overall view of the financial services harmonization process from the perspective of an 'agnostic'.

First, the most remarkable features of the Commission Proposals will be described, as well as the opinions of high-level civil servants of the Commission staff regarding the achievement of an internal market for financial services in 1992. Second, a critical analysis will be made, regarding issues which, it may be suggested, have not been correctly focused on by the Commission proposals. The final outcome of this approach should contribute to the general conclusions of the book, mostly as regards the legal issues at stake for the achievement of an unified banking market within the 1992 Single Market.

The Commission Proposals for the Achievement of a Unified Financial Market

The Single European Act (SEA) set both the objectives[1] and the date[2] for the creation of an area without internal frontiers in which the free movement of goods, persons, services and capital would be guaranteed. Article 13 of the SEA (8 A of the EEC Treaty) gave formal recognition to the objectives included within the Commission's White Paper for the achievement of the internal market,[3] which included the main guidelines for the integration of the European financial markets.

The Commission proposals to create a single market in financial services have two main components. The first is the complete liberalization of capital movements.[4] The second is the opening up of the market for financial services by removing barriers to the cross-border marketing of financial services and the free circulation of financial products. The general method of achieving those objectives is as follows. On the one hand is the harmonization of key standards for the prudential supervision of financial institutions and for the protection of investors, depositors and consumers. The White Paper talks of minimum standards covering: solvency, fitness and properness, disclosure of information to clients and consumer protection through guarantee funds. On the other hand is the introduction of a single licensing system for financial institutions, based on mutual recognition and home country control.

From a formal perspective, the Commission's approach for the completion of the financial services unified market is coherent with that for the completion of their internal market. The internal market programme is surreptitiously linked to deregulation. The logic of the internal market is that, without borders, resources and products will be more effectively allocated through the Community thereby creating a global increase of wealth. This leads, more or less directly – according to the personal ideology and degree of social awareness of the thinker – to the idea that geographical distortions cannot be supplanted by sectoral ones in order to hold back the 'allocative efficiency' of the market throughout the Community. In this sense, the liberalization of financial services in Europe means not only the disappearance of geographical barriers, but also sectoral and communitarian ones. Perhaps the deregulation approach underlying the Commission proposals is due to the Commission's view of 'political feasibility'. When possible, Community institutions will try to avoid changes in legislation, a consequence of the subsidiary communitarian principle – a principle found in the Delors Report which holds that the Community should only assume competencies in areas where Community authority is more efficient than national regulation.

Thus, three primary ideas of the Commission – integration, deregulation and political feasibility – are the basis of the internal market programme concerning financial services.

The minimum harmonization approach of the Commission White Paper aims to set up minimum requirements to be accomplished by banks. Although national authorities can settle more demanding requirements, this would entail a negative competition position for their national banks, but an equal protection of users of financial services since these will be provided abroad. Therefore, there is no other consequence but the deregulation of financial services throughout the EC, since countries will probably set up national standards as demanding as the minimal standards of Community Directives.

The texts where those principles have been settled emphasize the importance of preserving financial stability while avoiding any kind of barriers to the free provision of financial services and the free establishment of financial entities.[5] This 'spirit' is largely confirmed by the opinions of Commission civil servants.[6]

Fitchew remarks that the Commission's aims are in line with the examples of 'deregulated financial markets elsewhere in the world'.[7] 'We shall have a liberalized market in the sense that we shall be open to the rest of the world ...'.[8] Other features of importance noted by Fitchew are related to the legal approach for the achievement of the Commission objectives.[9] Priorities have been settled on problems relating to 'mass risks', insurance (due to the ageing population in Europe), capital adequacy rules for banks and other investment business, 'public interest' restrictions and the partial harmonization of 12 different systems of contract law.[10] However, Fitchew recognizes that the Commission proposals will not achieve complete uniformity of market conditions by 1 January 1993, but that some of these differences are going to be removed '... either by the eroding forces of competition or by actions before the Court or by further harmonization ...'.[11] Thus, the question arises of why the full harmonization of tax regimes, consumer protection and contract law – all of great importance in banking – have not been conceived as priorities to be achieved by Community legislators. Because of this, the full implications of 1992 will differ with respect to 'wholesale' and 'retail' banking. As regards the Commission's proposals, the implications for the 'wholesale' market should be greater, but, so far as 'retail banking' is concerned, we shall view the Community as a collection of 12 nation states rather than as a single market. If things remain as they are, then 12 sets of products will continue to have 12 separate sets of costs, with minimal benefits to the consumer from economies of scale.

Sutherland considers the creation of 'financial supermarkets' to be the most relevant feature to be achieved by the Commission proposals.[12] This idea is directly linked to the concept of dismantling the specialization rules and the compartmentalization of European financial markets. Many of the restrictions on who could do what and on what kind of financial investment could be bought and sold will be removed.[13]

Clarotti stresses the importance of several factors. The first is internationalization: the rules intending to be applied at the European financial market have to be in accordance with those of the world financial market. Second is the achievement of the deregulatory objectives throughout 'Recommendations' rather than Directives in the near future, and third is the emphasis on 'liberalization'.[14]

The Commission proposals relied heavily on the study undertaken by Cecchini on 'The Cost of Non-Europe'.[15] For the purposes of the economic analysis undertaken by Cecchini and his team of experts, the three types of market barriers, which were identified in the 1985 White Paper, were regrouped into five categories: tariffs, quantitative restrictions (quotas), cost-increasing barriers, market-entry restrictions and market-distorting subsidies and practices. As regards financial services, the benefits to be achieved by the integration of the European financial markets will be: commercial loans (19.2 million ecu); consumer credits (38.5 million ecu); credit cards (25.7 million ecu); mortgages credits (118.8 million ecu); travellers' cheques (29.6 million ecu); currency exchange (196.3 million ecu); others (58.9 million ecu). Total profits for consumers ('retail banking') will be around 3.189 million ecu.[16] At first sight, these data seem very impressive – a reaction apparently shared by the Commission civil servants. However, there are many opinions which contradict the conclusion of the Cecchini report.

The above analysis summarized all of the Commission proposals for the creation of a European financial area. Therefore, both the spirit and the flesh of this European institution, as regards the banking harmonization process in Europe, must be analysed within the context above. As Jacques Delors expressed in a 'note' to the President of the Council:

> It remains that, in the field of banking at least, the Commission considers that the directives which have already been adopted, those which it has presented to the Council and those which it has announced, form a body of texts sufficient to ensure the effective freedom to provide services ....[17]

Current developments on European financial legislation do not seem to pave the way for so many 'congratulations'.

A Critical Analysis of the Commission Proposals

The internal market forces the EC to make four fundamental choices: on the nature of the financial market, on the coherence of a system of 'home country control' for 12 Member States, on the level of financial security and on the prudential and fiscal rules required.

But scholars do not seem too convinced so far as the technical foundations of the Commission's planning for the achievement of an integrated financial area is concerned. Both the legal and the economic approaches of the Commission have received criticism, the common core of which is the lack of a coherent schedule as regards the consequences of the above approach on different socioeconomic fields.

First, we shall analyse the criticism of the legal aspects of the foundations of the financial harmonization process. Usher does not share the

White Paper emphasis on the free circulation of financial products equated to that of the free movement of goods:

> ... the fundamental problem with financial services ... is that what is on offer is a continuing legal relationship, the very nature of which may be dependant upon the local legal system.[18]

Baltensperger and Dermine say that the European Commission, despite adopting the principle of home country control for banking supervision, has proposed the national treatment principle for deposit insurance, which could create stability problems for the financial systems and hinder the prevention of a systematic crisis, leading to the default of solvent banks.[19]

Mutual recognition is criticized by Vasseur as regards the inclusion of activities not banking 'sensu stricto', within the annex to the Second Banking Directive (bonds issues, securities and real state management, financial advice, and so on). This situation is likely to create future problems related to the recognition of the activities by countries in which regulations could exclude some of them from banking.[20]

The nature of the entire financial services harmonization process is also questioned by other scholars. McGee and Weatherhill lent weight to the above critics by maintaining that the Commission's 'New Approach' to the removal of lawful technical barriers to trade follows the essence of the Court's Cassis de Dijon approach to unlawful barriers, in that the emphasis is on general objectives not precise details, which establishes 'a uniform community standard of which the precise content is left inexplicit'.[21] But their most important remark is about the relationship which they establish between the Commission deregulatory strategy and a policy of privatization. Warnings about the consequences of this approach are also given: first, about the lack of attention to the interests of all affected parties within the system to be created; second, about the control by business groups of the standard-setting process; third, about the shaping of future legislation, in the sense that business interests will block consumer protective initiatives.

Vitale relates the legal nature of the Banking Directives to the neoliberal ideology looking for the lowest regulatory common denominator.[22] In this sense, Capotorti is especially critical as regards the legal 'vacuum' in the Commission's conception for the achievement of the financial market.[23] Micossi emphasized this view, remarking that the task of Community legislation is narrowed to the 'identification' of a platform of common standards.[24] De Boisseu warns about future risks arising from the 'position risk' of the credit institutions (linked to tax fluctuations, exchange tax and the like), and which are not included within the Cooke ratios – the ones adopted by the Commission's proposals.[25] Dornbusch thinks that the Commission's strategy to proceed with liberalization 'no matter what' could be harmful, rather than helpful, to European integration.[26]

In Van den Bempt's fiscal disallocation, as well as financial disallocation, are risks which could arise in future, due to the Commission approach which gave priority to the liberalization of capital movements rather than to the fiscal harmonization of financial fluctuations.[27]

Tillet expresses doubts as regards the conduct of business regulation within the Commission's proposals. Despite the fact that the principles of mutual recognition and home country control would increase competition among the different national regulatory systems,[28] by no means would they deprive national regulators of all discretion. Host countries would oversee risk-taking in the securities markets, control bank liquidity and set monetary policy. Thus, Tillet thinks that difficulties will arise because the conduct of business rules will be laid down by one authority but will be enforced by another.[29]

Therefore the linkage to any 'communitarian principle, sensu strictu' seems to be far from clear. What really matters to European regulators is to confront the issue of devising more stringent regulatory and enforcement modalities to take account of the breaking down of the segmentation of localized markets. London thinks that the Commission's proposals cannot be understood as intrinsically enacted for the achievement of the 'final stages' but as 'transitorial' measures. If the Single European Act does not embody any new competencies for the European institutions in the monetary field – and, as said before, the White Paper measures have been embraced by the SEA – the completion of the financial services harmonization process must be viewed in a short- to medium-term perspective.[30] Therefore, the Commission presented a set of proposals aiming to adapt existing regulations to some of the new problems created by the development of the financial services markets in the Community.

The completion of the planning for the achievement of a legal environment within which EC citizens could profit from a more efficient financial market seems to be just a 'fairy tale'. The adoption of principles and techniques which could work in other sectors (such as the free movement of goods), or which have been shaped for a global market, gives the impression that 'the harmonization of financial services' is the 'Cinderella' of the whole set of rules aiming to harmonize other fields within the EC.

As regards the Commission's economic approach, criticisms have been made of both the methodology and the principles underlying the building of the integrated financial market.

Wyplosz expresses disappointment with the use of the Cecchini report for many reasons. First, it is a 'microeconomic' study[31] whose conclusions cannot fail to have macro-economic implications. Second, from a macroeconomic point of view, it fails to separate the implications for the goods markets and those concerning financial markets. Third, the growth-enhancing effect is attributed to the supply side of the economy, without having in mind the influence of the demand side behaviour over the growth-enhancing effect.[32]

Bishop disagrees on the final benefits for consumers, unless there is sufficient 'currency stability' to make it practical to manufacture European-scale financial products:

> ... currency stability will be seen as an essential prerequisite to obtaining the extra scale of output from an industry whose raw materials is that currency.[33]

Andreu notices the fact that the Price Waterhouse study analysed 16 financial products (seven from banking) within several EC countries, which differs from the technique used by the OECD study (Revell, 1980), which arrived at different conclusions. Thus, the final outcome of the Price Waterhouse study is not too reliable.[34]

Hoffmeyer says that the analytical material provided by Price Waterhouse (based primarily on a comparative static analysis) illuminates actual price differences but provides little evidence on two important aspects: first, the distinction between retail and large transactions;[35] second, the shape of the 'penetration curve' – that is, the time needed and the final effect of opening up for more competition. He maintains that, while the biggest impact (that on large transactions) has already occurred, the penetration into retail transactions will probably be extremely slow, if any.[36] This means that the Cecchini report implies some methodological problems. First, the prices quoted do not represent actual consumer cost. Second, differences in the definitions used create discrepancies between the estimates for gains in consumer surplus for the entire credit sector. Third, cross-subsidization between financial products may often occur, which will obviously distort any figures. Fourth, it is possible that the countries with the lowest expected price reductions could, instead, actually face price increases as cross-border demand for their products rose.

As regards other economic implications of the Commission's approach, De Bossière thinks that the pattern to be created by the achievement of the White Paper's objectives will much more resemble a free trade area for capitals than to a Common Market.[37]

On the other hand, distortions could be expected as regards savings. If the division, currently existing within the EC, over the issues of withholding tax and bank secrecy remains after 1992, wealthy individuals will be tempted to place their savings in any country but their own, leading to a large distortion of savings patterns.

Last, but not least, Norup argues that the White Paper's set of rules for financial services will not, in themselves, bring along any considerable macroeconomic alterations. Therefore growth will not be as strong as the EC Commission assumes.[38]

Other issues which are worth mentioning concern social policy and fiscality, neither of which have been considered directly by the Commission approach.

The impact of the Single Market on employment in the sector is as yet uncertain. Financial services is an industry that relies heavily on a highly-skilled workforce. The ferocity of competition for skilled employees may increase and may also lead to redundancies and a decline in job security in some areas.[39]

The absence of any achievement in the mortgage credit field, within the Community strategy, should also be noted. The creation of a single market for financial services will favour universal banking whilst neglecting specialized banking. As housing is one of the major social policy aims, mostly for less well-off citizens, the damage to the human face of the single market is a fact.[40]

On the other hand, it is worth questioning why the Commission proposals do not take into account some of the developments within the company law field, as regards both the participation of workers in the profits of the credit institutions and in their administrative councils. If the proposals place the accent on 'asset profitability' – that is, opening the door for cost accounting and economic analysis in banks, and leading them to review their development strategy in the same terms as any commercial enterprise – why not do the same as regards workers' participation.[41] In this sense, it is also striking that the Commission took no account of the Kirchner report[42] which called for the extension of industrial democracy and recognized that union–employer relations will also have to undergo change, nor of the 1980 OECD report in which retail banking was seen as a high-cost area because of the level of investment required in human and material resources, which banks were seeking to cut.[43] Retail banking (bank branching) is currently threatened by both new technology (provision of electronic points of delivery) and customer behaviour (self-service).[44] This situation will foster some of the problems for branching expansion after 1992, which are the huge costs of establishing a market presence, changing local customs and habits or people's preference for familiar names and institutions, all of which do not contribute to the creation of jobs.

Some observations must be made about fiscal issues. Taxation differences preoccupy many of those involved in financial services. The lack of Community proposals for the harmonization of such matters as withholding tax on dividends and interest,[45] as well as in financial transactions,[46] could provoke distortions concerning the placement of capital investments, depending on the fiscal treatment given by the different Member States. So far as saving fiscality is concerned – a matter of concern for the majority of citizens up to now – agreement has been reached only as regards 'cooperation' between the Member States, but the problem of double taxation is still unsolved.[47]

Notes

1 OJ L 169, 19/6/1987, specially articles 13–19.
2 It is worth noting that declaration no. 3 of the SEA states as not legally binding the date of 31 December 1992 for the completion of the internal market.
3 COM (85); 310 final; Bull, C.E., no. 6, 1985.
4 See COM (86), 326 final, and Directive 86/566 EEC, OJ L 332, 26/11/1986.
5 See Commission of the ECs: *Completing the Internal Market: an Area without Internal Frontiers. The Progress report required by article 8B of the EEC Treaty*; 17 November, 1988.
6 A very good example of this 'spirit' is the content of UCITS Directive of 22 June 1987; O.J. no. L 185 of 7 July 1987.
7 See G. Fitchew, 'Overview. European Financial Markets: The Commission's Proposals' *European Banking in the 1990s*, London: Blackwell, 1990, p. 13.
8 Ibid.
9 See G. Fitchew, *The Progress to Date: An EC Perspective in Restructuring Europe's Financial Services, 1992 and Beyond*, Rooster, 1989.
10 Ibid., p. 9.
11 Ibid., p. 24 and p. 32.
12 See P. Sutherland, *1er janvier 1993: ce qui va changer en Europe*, Paris: Presses Universitaries de France, 1987.
13 The long list of activities for which the single banking licence would be valid is proof of this.
14 P. Clarotti, 'Le système bancaire européen' in *The European Integration of Financial Markets*, Maastricht, 1986, p. 11.
15 Commission of the EEC: *Research on the Cost of Non-Europe*, Luxembourg, 1988.
16 See pages 27 and 60–3 of volume 9 of *Research on the cost of non-Europe*, Price Waterhouse Financial Services, 1988.
17 See 'The note from the President of the Commission to the President of the Council', Informal meeting of the Ministers for Economy and Finance at Knokke, April 1987, last paragraph of point 3 (2).
18 See J. Usher, *1992 and the Implications for Banking and Finance. An Overview*, European Institute, University de Saarlandes, 1989. p. 3 et seq.
19 See E. Baltensperger and J. Dermine, *Prudential and Regulatory Issues, Economic Policy*, **4**, 1987, p. 18.
20 See M. Vasseur 'Les problèmes juridiques de L'Europe Financière, *La Revue Banque* (486), September 1988, p. 40 et seq.
21 A. McGee and S. Weatherhill, 'The Evolution of the Single Market Harmonisation or Liberalisation', *Modern Law Review*, **53**, 5 September 1990, p. 583.

22 P. Vitale, 'Introduction' to *L'attuazzione delle Direttive CEE in materia creditizia*, Milan: Giuffré Edit, 1983, p. 13.
23 See F. Capotori, 'Intervento Conclusivo' in P. Vitale, L'attuazione, ..., op. cit., p. 441.
24 S. Micossi, 'The Single European Market: Finance', *Banca Nazionale del Lavoro Quarterly Review*, **V XLI** (164–67) 1988, p. 217 et seq.
25 C. De Boisseu, 'Les raisons de la faillité bancaire', in *Le FIG-ECO*; cit. supra, p. 34.
26 R. Dorn Busch, 'Money and Finance in European Integration', mimeo, INSEAD, January 1988.
27 P. Van den Bempt, 'La fiscalité de l'épargne' within 'Les problèmes fiscaux liés à la libération des mouvements de capitaux et des prestations de services financiers' in *La création ...*' op. cit., p. 41 et seq.
28 These systems would be under great pressure to converge, since regulations that limit the ability of a country's own banks to offer certain products disadvantage those relative to banks from other EC countries that allow these products.
29 P. Tillet, 'Banking regulation and 1992' in *1992, The legal ...*, op. cit., pp. 43–59.
30 C. London, 'Le secteur bancaire au regard du droit communautaire' in *Revue Trimes du Droit Européenne*, **23** (4), October–December 1987; pp. 593–619.
31 The Single European Act is clearly a set of microeconomic policy measures.
32 C. Wyplosz, 'Asymmetry in the EMS: Intentional or Systemic?', *INSEAD Working Paper*, no. 88/41, Bologne, August 1988.
33 G. Bishop, 'The Progress to Date: Banking' in G. Fitcht (ed.), *Restructurating Europe's Financial Services*, op. cit., p. 41.
34 J.M. Andreu, 'La Banca y el futuro: un panorama complicado, *ICE* (2131), 2–8 May 1988, p. 1626. See also 'Los servicios financieros ante el mercado interior', *ICE*, 27 March, 2 April 1989, p. 1302. See also the opinion of Mr José Luis Leal (President of the AEB) on 'minimizing' the implications of 1992 for retail banking, mostly as regards the opening up of accounts by small savers in the EC, *El País* (Economía), 21 September 1991.
35 This is the difference in possibilities of substitutions for an individual person with connections with a single branch versus a big firm that has a broader choice.
36 See E. Hoffmeyer, 'Is there Over-optimism on European Financial Integration?', *Dammarks National Bank Monetary Review*, February 1989, pp. 19–24.
37 T. de Boissiere, 'Vaincre la fragmentation: une perspective generale d'un point de vue financier' in *The Internal Market for Financial Services*, Maastricht: EIPA 1987, p. 97 et seq.
38 P. Norup, 'Harmonisation and Liberalisation Efforts within the EEC with Particular Emphasis on the Danish Banking Environment', *Strategic Planning for 1992*, Butterworths and Eurofi. plc Ed., 1989, pp. 210–15.
39 See the Fifth Report of the Trade and Industry Committee, *Financial Services and the Single European Market*, London: House of Commons, Session 1988–89.
40 J. Rodríguez López and J.M. Salcedo Giner, 'Crédito especializado y mercado único'. El marco hipotecario de la CEE', *El País*, 7 February 1990. See also J. Rodríguez López, 'Liberalización Financiera y precios inmobiliarios', *El País*, 4 September 1991.
41 See A. Levy-Lang, 'Banking Strategies for the 1990s', in *Financial Institutions in Europe Under New Competitive Conditions*, Kluwer Academic Publishers, 1990, pp. 39–46.
42 Commission of the EEC: *Report on the Social Implications of Introducing New Technology in the Banking Sector*, Brussels, November 1983.
43 OECD Report, *Costs and margin in Banking: An International Survey*, 1980.
44 McKinsey Group, *Retail Banking Conference*, London, 1982.

45 See *The Single European Market: Survey of the UK Financial Services Industry*, London: Bank of England, May 1989. In the long term, free movement of capital and a single market in financial services may involve some loss of revenue to governments from this source.

46 Stamp duty, stock market, turnover tax, tax on insurance premiums, tax treatment of insurance catastrophe reserves and corporate taxation. See *Stamp duty and indirect taxes on transactions in securities in force in member countries of the European Community*, Committee of Stock Exchanges in the EEC, November 1988. Also *European Trends in Direct Taxation Towards 1992: Saving Tax Considerations as Applied to European Corporations* (3rd edn), Price Waterhouse, February 1989.

47 CA from Miss Scrivener of 30 July 1990. OJ, no. C-303/40 of 3 December 1990.

9 Conclusions

Several features have to be emphasized on the above analysis of the current 'deregulatory' environment of financial services in Europe.

First, the EC institutions have no choice but to develop a European policy based exclusively on European interests, which could help the achievement of an integrated financial area. Despite the successful achievement of European policy in other economic sectors (such as coal, steel, agriculture and fisheries) the financial services sector is far from an independent decision-making process. Decisions are taken in function of international developments within the financial markets.

Second, the institutional effort towards the creation of a European Central Bank lacks many of the foundations necessary to the shaping of an institution which could guarantee the implementation of public policy measures for the raising of European welfare standards.

Third, in recent decades, the international interdependence of the financial markets have been reinforced for the growth of the Euromarket. This situation affects both the independence of the national monetary authorities as regards its monetary policy capacity, and also the whole financial market's instability. For instance, the financial instruments created within the Euromarket foster the process of credit 'securitization' and, therefore also, that of the 'desintermediation' of the credit institutions. Thus, there is a risk that, in the near future, an uncontrolled flux of capitals towards the Euromarket could occur. This situation would imply a concentration of risks within the Euromarket and so could threaten the instability of the European financial markets.

Recent scandals regarding the behaviour of financial institutions should dispel any hesitation on the part of the current European regulators.

PART IV

GENERAL CONCLUSIONS

10 Introduction

This book concludes with some considerations which aim to embrace the whole range of fields with which the preceding analysis has been concerned: first, the socioeconomic environment influencing the above process; second, policy-making considerations regarding both the role of political decision-makers and the credit institutions' strategies for the achievement of their objectives; third, the consistency of the EC set of rules concerning the above-mentioned influences; and, fourth, the European financial landscape of the near future and its implications for other sectors of the Community life.

11 The Socioeconomic Environment

As legislative outcomes are very much influenced by the socioeconomic environment within which they have been shaped, it is worth noting some features of the current socioeconomic environment which, in my view, have influenced the EC regulatory strategy of banking activities:

1. The swing of the pendulum in favour of the 'invisible hand' has rendered obsolete national regulatory frameworks based on restrictions to capital flows or the provision of financial services.[1]
2. Banks have played the 'innovation' card to convince regulators to adopt 'deregulatory strategies fitting to the current socioeconomic environment' and to the globalization of the financial markets. But financial innovation only contributes modestly to progress in society as a whole.[2] The relationship between financial innovation and economic growth does not show a clear-cut interaction between the two variables.[3]
3. Three factors, which contributed to the above 'globalization' of the financial markets, must be noted. The first is the necessity to increase the monetary flux in order to avoid financial imbalances between world financial markets. Imbalances were created by both the oil crisis and the end of the gold convertibility of the US dollar. The second is the fluctuation of inflationary taxes within the economies of Western societies. The third is the development of telecommunications and informatics.

These features changed the face of the financial markets: markets grew to the detriment of the classic intermediary function developed by credit institutions. In other words, the macroeconomic environment reshaped the financial environment.[4] Credit institutions were confronted by a new situation which changed at least two aspects of their customary behaviour. First, companies went to the stock markets looking for cash, instead of borrowing through loans. Second, savers reduced their saving tax and reallocated their investments.[5] Credit institutions' strategies as regards the above changes were based on, at least, these points:

a The diversification of their activities.
b The innovation of their financial instruments adapting them to both the 'deflationist context' and the financial needs of companies and savers.
c Internal policies in order to reduce costs and risks, as well as a major concern about the state of their own funds and liquidity.[7]

The development of the above strategies established a new kind of credit institution. Their main features are progressive performance in the pattern of a universal bank and interpenetration in both the insurance and securities markets.[8]

The final outcome of this macro–microeconomic relationship can be clearly seen in the policy-making of Western countries' regulators (see below). Therefore, what underlies the current financial services regulation is a set of rules reflecting the internal credit institutions' strategies, adapted to an external macroeconomic context. This could explain why regulators have paid much more attention to 'suggestions' from the supply side of the market.

Thus, the socioeconomic environment influences the regulatory processes related to credit institutions, leaving little room for the inclusion of public policy considerations. There is no autonomous and independent programmation of the financial services regulations. Governments and the European institutions react to external factors, which often are imposed by an 'international context' which they cannot influence. Therefore, any kind of public policy consideration (as, for instance, consumers) is given a secondary place. This is not the case for credit institutions which, in general terms, are better prepared than citizens for adapting their 'profit-making' mentality to changes within the international context.

The skeleton of the process above can be outlined as follows: (A) given a market situation where credit institutions develop their activities under a given regulatory environment + (B) external factors change the above market situation + (C) credit institutions adapt their strategies to the new situations before the regulatory environment changes + (D) the new regulatory environment changes to reflect both the new external factors and the credit institutions' strategies, adapted to the new socieconomic environment.

Thus, the democratic aspect, as regards participation of citizens and trade unions in the set of financial regulations, is normally a very low priority. Legislation is enacted for conjunctural reasons, under the shadow of the credit institutions' interests.

Notes

1 See M. Vanheukelen and J. Pelkmans, *The European Integration of Financial Markets*, Maastricht: EIPA, 1986.
2 See J.A. Schumpeter, *The Theory of Economic Development*, New York: Galaxybook, 1961.
3 See R.W. Godsmith, *Financial Structure and Development*, New Haven: Yale University Press, 1969.
4 See W.I. Ethier and R.C. Marston (eds), 'International Financial Markets and Capital Movements', *Essays in International Finance*, Princetown (157), September 1985.
5 See M. Aglietta, 'Europe: la décennie de tous les dangers', *Doc. travail. CEPII* (85), 5 September 1985.
6 H. Geiger, 'Différences de structure et de competitivité dans les industries de services financiers en Europe' in proceedings of the *1986 symposium on Europe and the Future of Financial Services*, op. cit., pp. 37–55.
7 See J.C. Naouri, 'La réforme du finàncement de l'économie' Banque (459), March 1986. See also W. Silber, 'The Process of Financial Innovation', *American Economic Review*, May 1983.
8 P. Jaffre, 'L'unification du marché des capitaux', *Banque* (460), April 1986.

12 Policy-making Considerations

Regarding current developments of the financial markets regulatory outcomes of the Community, we ought to know in advance what 'financial policy', if any, the Community should establish in the near future. It is therefore worth noting some of the most important features within the decision-making process shaping the European financial environment. Some of the points to be stressed might answer some questions concerning why decision-makers have chosen a concrete set of rules, what factors have been taken into consideration for such decisions, and who, if anyone, is interested in the achievement of the objectives contained in the legal outcomes.

First, as regards the regulator's aims, we have to differentiate that of nationals from that of the Europeans. Economic and monetary policy may prove to be one of the policy areas which poses the sharpest supranational challenge in the run-up to 1992 and, to an ever greater extent, thereafter. Therefore, alone with business interest considerations, it is worth underlining some of those related to the surreptitious conflicts between national and European interets.[1]

Besides economic interests, to which we shall refer later, there is a more fundamental issue such as democratic control and the kind of monetary policy the Community might pursue. This issue is intimately linked to both the role and character of an EC Central Bank and the future direction of economic strategy.

As regards the EC Central Bank the political options are confronted between two neatly labelled factions: the monetarist anti-inflationists who believe that the EC Central Bank should be restricted to acting to counter inflation and ensuring monetary stability, and the neo-Keynesian supporters who believe that it should be used as a positive instrument of public policy.

A similar situation can be perceived concerning economic strategies. Conflicts thus arise because, while the EC institutions' dominant consensus is that decisions affecting growth, employment and living standards should be left to market forces, some of the Member States' governments comprise more interventionist-minded economic strategists, who think that the

EC Central Bank should modify free-market forces rather than act merely to reinforce them.

The institutional outcome of the above conflicts is the lack of any significant draft outlining the method by which the Economic and Monetary Union is going to achieve the aims for which it was conceived. This situation could be resolved by entrusting to the organs of the Community the definition and the implementation of short-term economic policy. This would entail giving the Community the right to prohibit inappropriate uses of policy instruments by Member States.[2]

Socioeconomic issues greatly influence the policy-makers' aims.[3] Among the factors to which financial services are reacting we can note, for example, the ageing population in Europe, European industrial restructuring, and the Japanese interest in the European market.

1 *The ageing population in Europe*:[4] The latest available projections indicate a rise of only 1.8 per cent in the population of the Community by the end of the century. This situation will have some consequences. First, as regards longevity, we can expect to see almost 6 million octogenarians by the year 2000. Second, the ratio of employed to retired people will fall significantly. Third, social security programmes for the provision of a secure retirement income for EC citizens are going to be affected. In 1985, 2.3 working people were available to support one retired person; in 2035 this is predicted to fall to 1.6 working people. As a result, governments will almost certainly be unable to fund their social security programmes:

> all over Europe governments are now moving towards the positive encouragement of personal financial planning as their actuaries predict certain bankruptcy if they attempt to continue to fund existing programmes from their reducing work forces[5]

Thus, the shift of responsibility from the state to the private financial institutions to secure citizens' standards of living in retirement seems inevitable.

2 *European industrial restructuring*: Another major source of new demands for financial services has been from the process of multinationalization of corporate business.[6] To preserve business relations with multinational enterprises, financial institutions had to strengthen their presence in foreign markets, which has favoured the spread of particular lending and funding techniques. This situation provoked government action aiming to promote the efficiency of financial markets by fostering innovation and reducing structural rigidities.

This strategy is rather difficult to implement and cannot be pursued by any government on its own. It implies a unity of intent and a real will of cooperation among different regulatory authorities. Thus, the strengthening of the prudential regulation and the harmonizing of supervision is lagging behind the evolution of the market.[7]

3 *Japanese interest in the European market*: To date, American investment in Europe is far greater than Japan's[8] but whether things will stay that way is another matter. Last year, the Japanese comfortably outstripped America in terms of mergers and acquisitions in Europe.[9] This situation contributes to the enhancement of the 'globalization' trend, the emergence of which has led the global players in the leading financial companies to establish their operations in strategic positions within Europe. In addition, Japan has become the world's leading creditor nation, fulfilling the role of supplying capital flows to the entire world economy.

As stated above, the multinationalization of commercial activities by European companies created a need for more capital and, in many cases, a wider shareholder base. Japan has made a major contribution in this area by facilitating capital flows.

The change to 'positive reciprocity' from 'negative reciprocity' within the Second Banking Directive provides an example of how much European governments influenced policy-making, in order to preserve the Japanese capital flow to the 'Fortress Europe' which is to be created by the completion of the White Paper rules for the achievement of the internal market.

Besides the above three issues, a passing mention should be made concerning citizens' saving habits. Within the current decade two principal changes can be highlighted. The first is the reduction of the saving tax which small investors used to save. The second is the shift of retail banking customers' investment tax towards both insurance and qualified financial instruments (as UCITS). These changes enhanced the 'despecialization' banking pattern (closely linked to the German *Allfinanzbanking*), rendering obsolete specialized credit institutions' market strategies. Thus, the above market situation has also influenced policy-makers when shaping the current regulatory environment.

Some considerations on the influence of socioeconomic issues on policy makers' strategies can be drawn from the above analysis:

1 It seems clear that the momentum of international deregulation and innovation is such that it is important for monetary authorities to take an active interest in deregulation accompanied by appropriate supervisory measures.

2 If 'deregulation' is the option to be developed by policy-makers in the immediate future, regulators should disclose what social benefits – in terms of wealth increases – can be expected from some of the factors underlying 'deregulatory' policies – for instance, financial innovations or stock exchange globalization.
3 Should profit margin increases be reinvested in the creation of companies, research, or technology? Should the above policy-making be not just efficient in itself, by its own measurement, but also play a role which is efficient for the economy as a whole?
4 Does deregulation really imply a decrease in the current prices of 'retail banking' financial products, affecting (as consumers) the majority of EC citizens? Or does it mean more speculation and wealth concentration for a limited number of market players sharing the monopoly rents which exist within it, rather than driving prices down?
5 We should question the relationship between policy-makers and credit institutions. To put it in a nutshell, are policy-makers sufficiently free to shape a financial environment of which its most important forces are not under their control? If, as stated above, not even social security expenses can be afforded by governments, or if, for instance, electoral campaigns are funded with loans from credit institutions, we would be sceptical about policy-makers' capabilities to shape a banking policy based on the public interest.

The European decision-making process shares the above features as regards the policy-makers' attitude towards banking regulations. Therefore, the EC legislative outcome permits several criticisms. First, it is very difficult to create a European financial regulatory environment when some of the factors shaping it are not specifically European – such as, for example, all the factors contributing to the 'globalization' of financial markets or the nature of the activities currently being developed by the European financial institutions.

Second, the legitimacy of the decision-making process is far from clear. Unless means are found of explaining the way in which the Community has developed the financial services decision-making process, we run the risk of triggering off national, regional and sectoral opposition to Community rules, which will certainly be costly. Lack of transparency and control are factors contributing to a 'democratic deficit' which is unacceptable in terms of the EC's foundations. The singularity of the 'small credit institutions community', as regards their influence on its own functioning regulation, makes a reality of Hirsch's statement that, except where control is attempted in small communities, this gives the controlled ample scope to manipulate information so as to escape restrictions.[10]

Third, with regard to the EC set of rules for the achievement of the integrated financial market, we notice the absence of proposals in a number of areas which are of great importance to the financial sector. There is little or no harmonization in areas such as company law, taxation, consumer protection and the like. As the problems in banking reflect problems elsewhere (in financial markets generally, in the property and labour markets) the absence of regulation in the above fields will drive monetary authorities to devise more complex, or more coercive, means of controls. This will provoke a paradoxical situation: while markets and market forces press towards deregulation regulators will probably apply, in function of the context, more stringent regulations. This confirms the theory that the EC has no common design for the shaping of the financial environment.

All these above considerations raise the question of who might benefit from a regulatory environment where many issues have still to be regulated. As we have seen, deregulation has been put forward by policy-makers as a standard solution to the complexities of exercising public control over financial markets. By retreating from intervention, regulators can certainly abandon the search for solutions, but they cannot, in so doing, abolish the opportunism which is at the heart of the policy problem. Opportunistic behaviour by powerful private interests is a key problem which European policy-makers have fostered with current deregulatory strategies for the financial markets.[11] In a recent report from *Euromoney*,[12] some of Europe's leading bankers expressed their views on current EC regulatory strategies.[13] The opinions showed that bankers were prepared for the current regulatory changes. Therefore, it may be stated that credit institutions are the best positioned to face the changes to be introduced by the set of rules enacted for the EC within the European financial environment.[14] In addition, the banks' position will be reinforced by the 'synergic interaction' of the less common-denominator regulatory strategy of the EC.

The theory of the 'opportunistic niches' (developed by economists)[15] fits the banks' behaviours within the EC regulatory strategies: 'loopholes' exist with respect to the many issues affecting banking behaviours which have not still been regulated by the EC and allow credit institutions to develop their profit-making strategies without any regulatory obstacle. Thus, the escalation of the current EC regulatory strategies regarding financial markets can be outlined as follows:

1 Four objectives are to be achieved by the EC regulatory strategies:
   - increasing welfare and protection standards for consumers (the first).
   - the facilitation of the provision of services to the producers (the second).

  - public policy considerations: both national and European interests as regards the instability of the financial system.
  - third country interests.
2. The above objectives have to be balanced by decision-makers in order to shape a policy which satisfies each of the interests at stake.
3. When the financial environment changes, policy-makers must regulate the new environment for public policy reasons.
4. 'Changes' are then used opportunistically by 'producers' for the shaping of the new regulatory outcomes.
   In the European environment, policy-makers have always favoured the producers for at least two reasons:
   a because the rules to be applied to the new financial environment fit with the producers' strategies,
   b because rules leave a wider room for market forces to play than for interventionist policies to act.
5. The final 'outcome' establishes a new hierarchy as regards the 'income' objectives:
   - European interest is subordinated to third countries' interests, acting through the globalization of the financial markets.
   - National interests are not sufficiently strong to shape the European financial environment. Not the English, nor even the Germans, have submitted a unitarian design for the shaping of the European financial environment.
   - Producers' interests lie with the globalization of financial markets. They are therefore in line with those of the third countries' credit institutions.
   - Consumers (citizens) have to deal with a set of regulations where their interests have not been taken into consideration.

We can therefore conclude by saying that, as regards financial services, the European policy-makers have given proportionally much more consideration to the interests of the economic supply side than to any other interests. The analysis of the EC regulatory outcome on the subject, given in Chapter 11, will help to confirm this statement.

Notes

1 See J. Palmer, *1992 and Beyond*, Luxembourg: Commission of the EEC, 1989.
2 See C. Segre, *La coordination des politiques de conjoncture dans La CEE*, Brussels: IEE (ULB), 1967.

3 See Levitt 'The Progress to Date: Investment Services', in *Restructuring Europe's Financial Services*, op. cit., note 24, p. 85 and note 9, p. 97 above.
4 See H. Thomas, 'The Changing Pattern of European Investment' in *Strategic Planning for 1992*, op. cit. Chapter 8, note 38, above, pp. 227 et seq.
5 Ibid., p. 229.
6 See 'Recent Innovations in International Banking', *BIS*, April 1986.
7 See M. Onado, 'New products and New Markets' in proceedings of the *Europe and the Future of Financial Services*, op. cit. pp. 691 et seq. See also C. Tugendhat, 'Opening up Europe's Financial Sector to Intra-Community Competition', *The Banker*, January 1985, pp. 21–5.
8 See 'The Changing Face of European Investment', *Business Life*, BA Magazine, October 1991.
9 For instance, they clocked up $5,6. billion, $3,9 billion of it in the UK. On the other hand, monthly trade figures show Japan's surplus with the EC is soaring into the two-billion-dollar territory.
10 F. Hirsch, *Social Limits to Growth*, London: Routledge & Kegan Paul, 1977, pp. 139, 131 and 143.
11 See C. Perrow, *Complex Organisations: a Critical Essay*, Glenview: Scott Foreman, 1972, pp. 1–60.
12 Special supplement, April 1991.
13 Those of the BNP, Credit Lyonnais, Crédit Agricole, Deutsche Bank, Commerzbank, DG Bank and Banco Ambrosiano Veneto.
14 See F.H. Juvigny, 'Les Pouvoirs Publics Français et des Résistances à la Création d'un Marché Bancaire Intérieur Unifié' in *Financial Institutions in Europe Under New Competitive Conditions*, Kluwer Academic Publishers, 1990, pp. 83–94. See also D. Tulasne, 'The Banker's Role in Europe Today and Tomorrow' (forthcoming).
15 See, among others G. Stigler, 'The Theory of Economic Regulations', *The Bell Journal of Economics and Managerial Science*, **2**, 1971; R. Savings-Thomas, 'Concentration Ratios and the Degree of Monopoly, *International Economic Review*, **11**, 1970; D.E. Lilienthal, *Big Business: A New Era*, New York, 1953; F.M. Scherer, *Industrial Market Structure and Economic Performance*, Chicago, 1980.

13 The Regulatory Outcome of the European Institutions

Current Trends

Two considerations have to be made with regard to what the Community has harmonized and what is to be harmonized. The principal items which have been harmonized are:

- the definition of what constitutes a credit institution;
- the calculation of ratios to establish banks' solvency liquidity and profitability;
- the annual accounts;
- supervision on a consolidated basis;
- the obligation for supervisory authorities to cooperate and exchange information;
- the requirement that all banking businesses be licensed;
- the indication of minimum licensing criteria.

Partial agreement as regards minimum levels have been achieved for:

- prior licensing requirements;
- requirements in respect of major shareholders of banks;
- deposit insurance (Recommendation);
- large exposures limitations (Recommendation).

Measures still remain to be taken on very important aspects, such as:

- rules on participation in non-bank activities;
- rules on ensuring compliance with home country's (secrecy) rules;
- rules on links between banking and insurance industries;
- links between banking and the securities industry, and bank holding companies.

This non-exhaustive list of harmonization measures gives an overall view of the Community's principal achievements in the regulation of financial services. From this, we can see that only some of the main issues affecting credit institutions' activities have been harmonized (more precisely, only those issues for which the financial institutions were prepared). The other items – all of great importance for the maintenance of current (and future) strategies of the largest players in the financial markets – are still to be harmonized. Only the purely 'technical' aspects connected with the industrial structure of the financial services sector have been harmonized through Directives of which the adoption procedures are protacted – and the actual points at which decisions are taken are not clear. For the remaining issues the Community has adopted a 'wait and see' approach, in the hope that many of the problems will be solved by the market itself.[1]

Second, as regards the legal instruments used to harmonize the above issues, the use of Directives, and the principles of home country control and mutual recognition, scarcely contribute to the achievement of a uniform regulatory environment and could create distortions and the maintenance of 12 different regulatory environments.

This is the result of the less well-defined concept of harmonization within the EC legal order. Community harmonization of policies is much more vague in practice, and much less well defined in the Treaty of Rome, than is generally believed. Thus, particular difficulty resides in attaining an overall approach to all major instruments for united objectives. Moreover, additional complexities arise from the absence of a will for collaboration between very strong national institutions, such as Central Banks and, sometimes, Ministries of Finance and the national economy. For this reason, it may be useful to consider the issues through private international law. On the basis of a Convention under article 220(3) of the EEC Treaty, Member States could provide a uniform answer to the many issues arising from the development of a common strategy for the regulation of financial services in Europe. This solution, which was conceived as being for company law harmonization by some scholars (for instance, Beitzke,[2] Stein[3] or Savatier[4]), despite the fact that it implies a slower decision-making process than by Directives, will have the additional advantage of providing a global view of what the Community must, or must not, regulate in the European interest. Additionally, it could be helpful for distinguishing 'liberalization' from 'harmonization', by stating in what areas 'liberalization' requires 'harmonization'. Unfortunately, historical experiences of the 1970s' projects for the enactment of a European Banking Law met with opposition from both governments and financial institutions. More than 20 years later we can perceive the same attitude within the European 'legal arena'.

Because financial institutions are developing the most important role within the current economic structures of Western societies. The implications of any regulatory strategy in this sector cannot be directly compared to any strategies regulating other economic sectors. Attitudes against transparency and control of the above regulatory processes by the citizens of so-called democratic societies threaten to breach the principal foundations of the Western countries' legal frameworks.

The European Financial Landscape of the Future: an Approximation from Today's Perspective

After 1992, Europe will need a rather long span of economic stability, enhanced by convergent and non-inflationary fiscal and monetary policies in order to adapt each of the Member States' economic structures to the new unified environment.[5] Therefore, governments' capability to regulate national markets will be shifted, through a cautious step-by-step process, to the European institutions. Thus, given the current 'dominant consensus' within the European institutions as regards economic policy strategies, market forces will become the decisive force behind economic growth and so, the future structure of financial institutions will be of great importance for all European citizens. In this sense we can note some of the features which will possibly affect the European landscape after 1992.

First, while the short-run effect of 1992 will increase competition in the financial services sector, without achieving benefits of scale, the long-run effect could be a reduction in the number of players.[6] This will be the 'regional' reaction to the world forecast of financial services behaviour, which says that, by the early part of the next century, there will be only some 20 international financial institutions dominating the world banking arena.[7] Thus, we can expect an oligopolitic market structure.

Second, if the interpenetration of credit institutions within other industrial sectors, mostly through the securities market, is going to continue as is currently happening[8] banks will hold the key to the most important factors for economic growth. Thus, taking into account that only some institutions will consolidate their economic influence in the near future, the decision-making targets will be concentrated in a small number of 'manager directorates'.

Third, if third countries' investment and cash flow to the European market is increasing, the European economy will reveal a dangerous face. National governments will have little capability to intervene whenever the market is unable to allocate efficiently the resources for the creation of wealth. European financial institutions will not have complete capability for the shaping of the economic environment, despite their privileged market situation, because of the existence of third countries' economic interests.

Fourth, as regards the financial services' current industrial structure, some changes can be forecast, mostly in respect of 'despecialization' and the creation of financial conglomerates. It seems probable that the largest banks dominating the banking sector will also dominate the above financial system through their participation in holding companies.

Notes

1 G. Fitchew, Presentation to Financial Times Conference, Venice, 16 May 1989.
2 'Zur Aner Kennung von Handelsgesellschaften in EWG-Beireich, in Aussenwirtschaftclienst des Betrieb-Beraters', 1968, pp. 91–99.
3 'Conflicts-of-Laws Rules by Treaty: Recognition of Companies in a Regional Market' in *Michigan Law Review*, 1970, pp. 1327–31.
4 'Le marché common au regard du droit international privé', in *Revue Critical de Droit International Privé*, 1959, pp. 237–44.
5 See M. Lusser, 'Don't Jump to (Monetary) Conclusions' in *European Affairs*, 1989, pp. 66–9.
6 See G. Bishop, 'The Progress to Date: Banking' in *Restructuring Europe's Financial Service, 1992 and Beyond*, pp. 8–10, op. cit. note 24, Chapter 7 above.
7 See W.G. McLuskie, '1992, A Corporate Treasurer's View', in *IBI*, 1992, *Planning for Financial Services and the Insurance Sector*, Butterworths and Eurofi plc., 1989, pp. 160 et seq.
8 See R.W. Goldsmith, *Financial Structure and Development*, Yale University Press, 1969, pp. 390–409. See also statistical data from A. Torrero Mañas, *Relaciones Banca–Industria*, Madrid: Espasa Calpe Editores, 1991.

14 Final Remarks

The European Community must establish a more coherent financial policy according to the main foundations of the EEC Treaty. It is far from clear whether wealth creation is a matter for the market forces concerned, or whether or not, industrial democracy contributes to enhance companies efficiency. It is unacceptable for 'key' decision-making processes, such as that of the financial services, should be maintained outside citizens' control. Indeed, despite its complexity, the financial markets need a wider presence of public regulators.

The whole of society must have the sensation that what is happening in the 'financial galaxies' is a question of public concern.[1] Submission to the wild play of market forces is not the most suitable way to achieve wider ranges of freedom and wealth. Therefore, any policy-making paving the way to 'self-regulation' seems to us merely second-best and it does not fit with the spirit of the EEC Treaty. 'Cooperation', 'solidarity' and 'democratic control' are some of the words that no policy-maker should ban from his dictionary. Any regulatory strategy within the EC must contribute to the concrete realization of those three essential concepts.

Note

1 See, again, the significance of stock markets crashes for the whole economic wealth of Western societies. In the last four years Wall Street has suffered three 'black days' (respectively on Fridays 16 October 1987, 13 October 1989 and 15 November 1991).

Selected Bibliography

Abellán, V. (1974), *Normas CEE y legislación española sobre establecimiento de personas Físicas y sociedades*, Madrid: JEA, pp. 22 et seq.

Abraham, J.P. and Triffin, R. (1987), 'L'Europe Financière', *Revue d'Economie Financière*, París (2) pp. 59–92.

Aldcroft, D.H. (1978), *The European Economy 1914–1970*, London: Croom Helm.

Angulo, E. (1987), 'La adhesión española a la CEE y la ordenación bancaria' in S. Martín Retortillo (ed.), *Estudios de Derecho Público Bancario*, Madrid: Ceura.

Asociación Española de la Banca, *Memoria 1988*, Madrid.

Averyt, W. (1975), 'Eurogroups, Clientele and the European Community', *International Organization*, **29** (4), Autumn, pp. 949–72.

Azqueta Oyarzun, P. (1982), 'La integración española en la CEE: repercusiones sobre el sistema financiero y el mercado de valores', *RIE*, **9**, pp. 509 et seq.

Balassa, B. (1975), *European Economic Integration*, Amsterdam: North Holland.

Balbus (1971), 'The Concept of Interest in Pluralism and Marxian Analysis', *Politics and Society*.

Banking Federation of the European Community (1988), *Annual Report*, (November 1986–December 1987), Brussels.

Barberm J. and Reed, B. (eds) (1973), *European Community: Vision and Reality*, London: Croom Helm.

Barnouin, B. (1986), *The European Labour Movement and European Integration*, London: Frances Pinter.

Bebr, G. (1959), 'The Balance of Power in the European Communities', *Annuaire European*, **V**, The Hague: Nijhoff, pp. 53–79.

Beever, R.C. (1960), 'European Unity and the Trade Union Movement', *Aspects Européens*, serie D. Etudes Sociales, Leyden: Sythoff.

Berger (1981), 'Introduction' in S.D. Berger (ed.), *Organizing Interests in Western Europe; Pluralism, Corporatism and the transformation of Politics*.

Bernard, N. Laval, C. and Nys, A. (1972), *Le Comité Economique et Social*, Brussels: VLB.

Bifulco, R. (1987), 'The liberalization of Banking Services' in *Journal of Regional Policy*, Naples, **7**, July-September, pp. 455–64.

Börner, (1965), 'Die Fünfte Freiheit des Gemeinsames Markets; Der Freie Zahlungsverkehr', *Zeitschrift für Ophüls* (199).

Bourgoignie, T. (ed.) (1989), *Electronic Fund Transfer Systems and Consumer Protection. Transferts électronique de fonds et protection du consommateur*, Brussels: Story-Sciencia.

Bourillon, C. (1963), 'Les progrès de la circulation des capitaix dans le Marché Commun', *Banque* (235), pp. 525 et seq.

Bowers (ed.), *Inflation, Development and Integration: Essays in Honour of A.J. Brown*, Leeds: Leeds University Press.

Boyer, A. 'Discriminationes tra le banche nella CEE', *BBTC*, **XLIV**, Part 1.

Bracewell-Milnes, B. (1976), *Economic Integration in East and West*, London: Croom Helm.

Bradandière, E. (1960), 'Banking in the Common Market', *Journal of the Institute of Bankers*, **81**, pp. 358–68.

Briquet, N. (1973), 'Premières mesures de libération pour les banques et les compagnies d'assurances', *Rev. MC*, pp. 463–65.

Brown, B.E. (1957), 'Alcohol and Politics in France', *American Political Science Review*, **51**, pp. 976–94.

Buchan (1988), 'EC Deeply Divided over Banking Reciprocity', *Financial Times*, 8 November, *European News*, p. 3.

Bureau Européen des Unions de Consommateurs (1988), *Achievement of a Common Market in Financial Services: Present State of EEC Measures*, BEUC/183/88, Brussels, October.

Butler, M. (1986), *Europe: More than a Continent*, London: Heinemann.

Butt, A. (1985), *Pressure Groups in the European Community*, London: UACES.

Butt, P. (1983), 'Pressure Groups and Policy-making in the European Community in J. Lodge (ed.), *Institutions and Policies of the European Community*, 1983, at p. 21.

Cairncross, A. *et al.* (eds), *Economic Policy for the European Community: The Way Forward*, London: Macmillan.

Campet, C. (1974), 'La libération de la activité bancaire dans la CEE', *Banque* (327), pp. 225 et seq.

Cecchini, P. (1989), *Europa 1992: Una Apuesta de Futuro*, Madrid: Alianza.

Clarotti, P. (1987), 'Comment batir l'Europe des banques. La reconnaissance mutualle, complement de l'harmonisation' in *Banque* (475), September, pp. 758–70.

Clarotti, P. (1982), 'L'armonizzazione dei bilanci delle banche sul piano comunitario', *BBTC*, **XLV**, Part 1: 'La coordination des législations bancaires', *Rev. MC* (254), pp. 71 et seq.

Coffey, P. (1979), *Europe and Money*, London: Macmillan.

Coffey, P., *Economic Policies of the Common Market*, London: Macmillan.

Coffey, P. (1987), *The EMS: Past, Present and Future* (2nd edn), Oxford: Oxford University Press.

Coffey, P. and Presley, J. (1971), *European Monetary Integration*, London: Macmillan.

Colombo, G.E. (1983), 'Le linee ispiratrice della proposta di direttiva comunitaria sui bilance dell banche', *BBTC*, **XLVI**, Part 1.

Commission of the EEC (1988), 'Research on the "Cost" of Non-Europe', Luxembourg 1988, **8**, *Business Services*, **16**, North America, Internal Market.

Costa, A. (1977), 'Problemi delle stabilimento e della prestazzione di servizi per le banche e gil altri istituti finanziari nella CEE' (Study in European Law in Honour of Riccardo Monaco), Milán, pp. 155–73.

Crabe, M., French, M. and Shale, T. (1988), 'Obscuring the 1992 Vision. A 1992 Banking Story That Won't Put You to Sleep' in *Euromoney*, June, pp. 29–31.

Creslet, W. (1987), 'La necessaire adpatation des banques espagnoles à la concurrence européenne' in *Problèmes économiques* (2035), 29 July, pp. 29–31.

Daltrop, A. (1982), *Politics and the European Community*, London: Longman.

Damm, 'Banking in the EEC', *Journal of the Institute of Bankers*, **9**, p. 369–77.

Dassesse e Isaacs (1985), *EEC Banking Law*, Lloyds: London.

Debunne, G. (1987), *les syndicates et l'Europe*, Paris: Editions Labor.

Dennis, G. (1985), 'The European Monetary System' in A.M. El-Agraa (ed.), *The Economics of the European Community*, Oxford: Philip Allan.

Denton, G. (ed.) (1969), *Economic Integration in Europe*, London: Weidenfeld and Nicholson.

Denton, G. (1974), *Economic and Monetary Union in Europe*, London: Croom Helm.

Denunne, G. (1987), *Les Syndicates et l'Europe*, Paris: Editions Labor.

Dettiènne, J. (1975), 'La liberté d'établissement des banques et des autres établissements financiers', *Revue de la Banque*, pp. 439 et seq.

Duverger, M. (1955), *Political Parties*, London: Methuen.

Economic and Social Committee (1980), *European Interest Groups and their Relations to the Economic and Social Committee*, Farnborough: Saxon House.

Edward (1987), 'Establishment and Services: an Analysis of the Insurances Cases', *EC Review*, **12** (23).

Eguidazu, S. (1985), 'La política bancaria comunitaria y las negociaciones de adhesión', *ICE* (620), pp. 50 et seq.

Ehrmann, H.W. (ed.) (1958), *Interest Groups on Four Continents*, Pittsburg: University of Pittsburg Press.

El-Agraa, A.M. (ed.) (1985), *The Economics of the European Community*, Oxford: Philip Allan.

Escande, J.P. (1987), 'L'harmonisation monetaire et financière au sein de la CEE' *JORF*.

European Trade Union Institute (1987), Info 21, *European Trade Union Confederation – Profile of the ETUC*, Brussels.

European Council for Payment Systems (1987), *European Accord for Bank Card Usage. Detailed Proposals for the Implementation of European Reciprocity, August.*

European Consumer Law Group (1988), *Arguments in Favour of Consumer Protection with Regard to the New Electronic Means of Payment*, Brussels, October.

Fitchew, G. (1988), *Completion of the Single Market in Financial Services*, Background Report of a briefing on 9 September 1988 at the London Office of the Commission of the EC (ref. ISEC/B16/88 of 10 October).

Flynn (1988), 'Insurance: Recent Judgements of the European Court', *ICLQ*, **154**.

Fontaine, A. (1961), 'L'Europe politique', *Revue du Marché Commun* (33), pp. 61–4.

Gavalda, C. (1974), 'La libération de l'établissement et des prestations de services bancaires dans la CEE', *Rev. Trim. D^{a} Europeo.*

Gavalda, G. (1974), 'Droit de la banque', *PVF* (36), pp. 695–707.

Gavalda, G. (1974), 'La première Directive de coordination des legislations bancaires de la CEE' (12.12.1977), *Rev. Trim. Dr. Europeo.*

Georges, S. (1985), *Politics and Policy in the European Community*, Oxford: Clarendon.

Giavazzi (1988), '*The EMS*', Cambridge: Cambridge University Press.

Gilb (1981), *Public or Private Governments*, P.G. Nystrom W.H. Starbuck (edts).

Goode, R. (ed.) (1985), *Electronic Funds Transfer: the Legal Implications*, London: The Institute of Bankers/Centre for Commercial Law Studies.

Goode, R. (1974), 'A Credit Law for Europe?', *ICLQ*, **23**, pp. 227–91.

Gortner, H.F. (1977), *Administration in the Public Sector*,

Grisoli, A. (1959), 'Integrazione Economica Europea ed unificazione del diritto', *RDC*, pp. 472 et seq.

Gurpide, J. (1989), 'La Europeización de la Banca Española', *El País*, November, December and January.

Haas, E.B. (1958), *The Uniting of Europe: Political, Social, and Economic Forces, 1950–1957*, Stanford: Stanford Press.

Haas, E.B. (1958), 'The Challenge of Regionalism', *International Organization*, **12**, pp. 440–58.

Haas, E.B. (1961), International Integration. The European and the Universal Process, *International Organization*, **15** (3).

Haas, E.B. (1964), *Beyond the Nation-State*, Stanford: Stanford University Press.

Hallstein, W. (1962), *United Europe: Challenge and Opportunity*, Cambridge, Mass: Harvard University Press.

Harrop, J. (1978), 'Convergence in Europe' in R. Wilson (ed.), *Workbook on Testing Ten Economies*, Sutton: Economics Association.

Henig, S. (1980), *Power and Decision in Europe*, London: Europotentials Press.

Herbe, R. (1985), 'Relations of Community Bureaucracy with the Socio-political Environment' in J. Jamar and W. Wessels (eds), *Community Bureaucracy at the Crossroads*, Bruges: De Tempel.

Hoffmeyer (1989), Is There Over-optimism on European Financial Integration?', *Danmarks Nationalbank Monetary Review*, February, p. 19.

Holt, S. (1967), *The Common Market*, London: Hamish Hamilton.

Holland, S. (1980), *Uncommon Market: Capital, Class and Power in the European Community*, London: Macmillan.

Hollensen (1988), 'The Establishment of the EEC Internal Market for Financial Services', *Danmarks Nationalbank Monetary Review*, **27** (11), August.

Hurtig, S. (1958), 'The European Common Market', *International Conciliation* (517), March, pp. 321–81.

Hutton (1972), *Banking in the EEC (Banking in Europe. The Challenge of Britain's Entry in the EEC)* London: Institute of Bankers, pp. 1–14.

Imbert and Fornsier (1986), 'Liberté de prestation de services et droit d'établissement, notamment en ce qui concerne les compagnies d'assurances et les banques', paper presented at the FIDE Congress, Paris.

Jacquemin, A.P. (1964), 'Size, Structure and Performance of the Largest European Firms', *The Three Banks Review*, June.

Jacquemin, A.P. and de Jong, H.W. (1977), *European Industrial Organisation*, London: Macmillan.

Jones, A.J. (1985), 'The Theory of Economic Integration, in A.M. El-Agraa (ed.), *The Economics of the European Community*, Oxford: Philip Allan.

Karlin (1989), La réglémentation prudentielle des banques', Part 2, **492**, *La Revue de la Banque* (269), March.

Keohane and Nye (1975), 'International Dependence and Integration', *International Politics* (Handbook of Political Science), **8**.

Key, S. (1985), 'Financial Integration in the EEC', International Finance Discussion Paper, Board of Governors of the FRS.

Kirchner, E.J. and Schawaiger, K. (1980), 'Interest Group Behaviour at Community Level' in L. Hurnitz (ed.), *Contemporary Perspectives on European Integration*, Westport: Greenwood Press, pp. 192–239.

Kirchner, E.J. and Schawaiger, K. (1984), 'The European Parliament and Interest Groups' in R. Hrbek, J. Jamar and W. Wessels (eds), *The European Parliament on the Eve of the Second Direct Election: Balance Sheet and Prospect*, Bruges: De Temple.

Kirchner, E.J. and Schawaiger, K. (1984), *The European Parliament: Performance and Prospects*, Aldershot: Gower.

Kirchner, E.J. and Schawaiger, K. (1986), *The Role of Interest Groups in the European Community*, Aldershot: Gower.

Korah, V. (1988), *EEC Competition Law and Practice*, Oxford: ESC.

Kruse, D.C. (1980), *Monetary Integration in Western Europe: EMU, EMS and Beyond*, London: Butterworths.

La Gaceta: Revista, Grupo Z (1989), *Un año de ajuste hace Europa: la Banca en el 89*, Madrid.

Langeheine, B. and Weinstock, U. (1985), 'Graduated Integration: A Modest Path Towards Progress', *Journal of Common Market Studies*, **23** (3), March.

Lapalombara, J.H. (1960), 'The Utility and Limitations of Interest Group Theory in Non-American Field Situations', *Journal of Politics*, **22**, pp. 29–49.

Lasok, P. (1988), 'Freedom to Provide Insurance Services' *MCR* (706).

Lasswell, H.D. and Kaplan, A. (1950), *Power and Society. A Framework for Political Inquiry*, Yale University Press.

Le Brun (1979) 'La première étape vers l'harmonisation européenes des réglementations bancaires', *Revue de la Banque*, **1**.

Lee, R. and Goden, P.E. (1976), *Economy and Society in the EEC*, Saxon House: Farnborough.

Lefpour A. and Y Lagumina, A. 'Banques Européennes: L'heure des rapprochement', *Entreprise* (819, 191), pp. 61–73.

Lindberg, L.N. (1963), *The Political Dynamics of European Economic Integration*, Stanford University Press.

Lindberg, L.N. and Scheingold, S.A. (1970), *Europe's Would-be Polity. Patterns of Change in The European Community*, Prentice-Hall.

Lipset, S.M. (1960), *Political Man: The Social Bases of Politics*, Welwyn Garden City: Doubleday.

López Roa, A. (1983), 'Crisis y transformaciones del sistema bancario español, *Boletín de Estudios Económicos*, **38**.

Louis, J.V. (1984), 'Free Movement of Tourists and Freedom of Payments in the Community', *CHLR*, **625.**

Lowi, T.J. (1979), *The End of Liberalism*, New York.

Ludlow, P. (1982), *The Making of the European Monetary System*, London: Butterworths.

Lukes, S. (1974), *Power: A Radical View*, London.

von Donat, M. (1979), *Europe: Qui tire les fuelles?* (trans.) Joos: LCD.

Maestreipieri, C. (1967), 'Noterelle sul diritto di stablimento e sulla libera prestazione dei Servici nella CEE, *Rev. Dir. Int. Pr. Proc.*, **3**, 1967, pp. 292–301.

Malvestiti, P. (1959), 'Les enterprises dans le Marché Commun', *Bulletin of the EEC* (3), pp. 5–17.

Mann (1982), *The Legal Aspect of Money*, Oxford: Oxford University Press, pp. 510–55.

Mattera, A. (1988), *Le Marché Unique Européen: ses Règles, son Fonctionnement*, Paris: Edit. JA.

Mendras, H. (1958), 'Méthodes, mouvements pour unir l'Europe', *Bulletin du Centre Européen de la Culture*, **6** (2), May.

Micossi (1988), 'The Single European Market: Finance', *Quarterly Review of the Banca Nazionale del Lavoro*, **165** (217), June.

Midland Bank (1977), 'European Monetary Union', *Midland Bank Review*, Winter.

Mimola, A.C. and Principe, A.C. (1983), *L'attuazione delle Directive CEE in materia creditizia*, Milan: Giufré.

Mitchell, J. (1987), 'Personal Financial Services in Europe: a Consumer Perspective', *Journal of Consumer Studies and Home Economics*, **11**, pp. 101–11.

Mitchell, J. (1988), *Electronic Banking and the Consumer: the European Dimension*; London: Policy Institute.

Mitrany, D. (1946), *A Working Peace System*, London and New York: Royal Institute of International Affairs.

Morgan Guaranty Trust (1988), 'Financial Markets in Europe: Toward 1992, *MGT Company World Financial Markets*, issue 5, September, p. 1.

Nigro, F.A. (1970), *Modern Public Administration* (2nd edn), Harper International edition.

Offe, C. (1975), 'The Theory of Capitalist State and the Problem of Policy Formation' in L.N. Lindberg, R. Alford, C. Cronch and C. Offe (eds), *Stress and Contradiction in Modern Capitalism: Public Policy and the Theory of the State.*

Oliver (1984), 'Free Movement of Capital', *Economic Law Review*, **9**, (401).

Olsen (1981), 'Integrated Organisational Participation in Government', in *Handbook of Organisational Design*, **2**, 'Remodelling Organisations and their Environments.

Oppermann, T. (1964), 'L'application des programmes géneraux de la CEE concernant la liberté d'établissement et libre prestation des services', *Rev. MC*, p. 556.

Owen, N. (1983), *Economies of Scale, Competitiveness and Trade Patterns Within the European Community*, Oxford: Oxford University Press.

Padoa-Schioppa, T. (1984), *Money, Economic Policy and Europe*, The European Perspective Series, Brussels: EC Commission.

Peters, B.G. (1984), *The Politics of Bureaucracy* (2nd edn), New York.

Peterson (1982), 'Capital Movements and Payments under the EEC Treaty', *EL Review*, **7** (167).

Pinder, J. (1987), 'Is the Single European Act a Step Towards a Federal Europe?', *The Journal of Policy Studies*, **7**, Part 4, April.

Pollard, S. (1974), *European Economic Integration 1815–1970*, London: Thames and Hudson.

Portales, G.B. (1982), 'Le Sucursali di banche stere', *BBTC*, 45, Part 1.

Postan, M.M. (1967), *An Economic History of Western Europe 1945–1964*, London: Methuen..

Presley, J.R. and Coffey, P. (1974), *European Monetary Integration*, London: Macmillan.

Presley, J.R. and Dennis, C.E.J. (1976), *Currency Areas: Theory and Practice*, London: Macmillan.

Pryce, R. (ed.) (1987), *The Dynamics of European Union*, London: Croom Helm.

Punset, E. (1981), 'El sistema bancario español ante le CEE', *ICE* (573).

Reich, N. (1988), 'Consumers and the Internal Market for Services: a Critique of "New Approaches" of the Community', unpublished, October.

Renda, B. (1972), 'Credito, Risparmio e banche nelle prospettive dell' integrazione europea', *Economie e Credito*, p. 19.

Robson, P. (1980), *The Economics of International Integration*, London: Allen and Unwin.

Roth, (1988), 'The European Economic Community's Law on Services: Harmonization', *Common Market-Law Review*, **25** (35).

Ruta, G. (1975), *Il sistema della legislazione bancaria* (2nd edn), Bancaria, pp. 158–62.

Sargent, J.A. (1982), 'Pressure Group Development in the EC: the Role of British Banker's Association', *In Journal of Common Market Studies* (3) March, pp. 185–269.

Sarnouin, B. (1986), *The European Labour Movement and European Integration*, London: Frances Pinter, 1986.
Scott (1989), 'La Notion de Réciprocité dans la Proposition de Dixième Directive de Coordination Bancaire', *Revue du Marché Commun* (323).
Schmitter (1979), 'Models in Interest Intermediation and Models of Social Change in Western Europe' in P.G. Schmitter and G. Lehmbruch (eds), *Trends towards Corporatism Intermediation*.
Schokking, J.J. and Anderson, N. (1960), 'Observations on the European Integration Process', *Journal of Conflict Resolution*, **4**, pp. 385–410.
Servais, D. (1988), *Un Espace Financier Européen*, Brussels: EC Commission.
Sharkansky, I. (1973), *Public Administration Policy–making in Governmental Agencies*, University of Wisconsin Press.
Sidjanski, D. (1984), 'Le Parlament Européen et les groupes d'intérêt' in R. Hrbek, J. Jamar and W. Wessels (eds), *The European Parliament on the Eve of the Second Direct Election: Balance Sheet and Prospects*, Bruges: De Temple.
Smits (1986), 'The End of Claustrophobia', *Economic Law Review*, **9**, (192).
Smits (1986), 'A further step on the road to liberalization?', *Economic Law Review*, **11**, (456).
Snyder, F. (1990), *New Directions in European Community Law*, London: Weidenfeld and Nicolson.
Stauder, B. (1986), *Les nouveaux moyens électroniques de paiement*, Lausanne: Payot, 1986.
Steffe, O. (1968), 'Analyse de la conjuncture et coordination des politiques conjoncturelles dans la CEE', *L'harmonisation dans les Communautés*, Brussels, pp. 194 et seq.
Stimmer (1985), 'EEC Freedom of Services and German Insurance Regulations', *Journal of Business Law*, p. 174.
Streeck and Schmitter (1981), 'Community, Market, State and The Prospective Contribution of Social Order', *Working Paper 91*, EUI.
Swann, D. (1985), *The Economics of the Common Market* (5th edn), Harmondsworth: Penguin.
Tarditi, S. (1984), 'Price Policies and European Economic Integration' in K.J. Thomson and R.M. Warren (eds), *Price and Market Policies in European Agriculture*, Dept. of Agricultural Economics, University of Newcastle upon Tyne.
Taylor, P. (1983), *The Limits of European Integration*, London: Croom Helm.
Termes Carrero, R. (1988), 'The Spanish Bank and the ECU" in *EBA Newsletter*, (3), January, pp. 29–34.

Thunis, X., Schauss, M. (1988), *Aspects juridiques du paiement par carte*, Brussels: Story-Scientia.

Toribio, J.J. (1981), 'La reforma financiera y el futuro de la banca', *Papeles de Economía Española* (7).

Tsoukalis, L. (ed.) (1986), *Europe, America and the World Economy*, Oxford: Basil Blackwell for the College of Europe.

Tsoukalis, L. (1977), *The Politics and Economics of European Monetary Integration*, London: Allen and Unwin.

Uriarte Santamaria, P.L. (1986), 'Banca y Comunidad Económica Europea' in *Boletín de estudios económicos*, pp. 29–46.

Usher (1981), 'Bank Charges and EEC Competition Law', *Journal of Business Law*, p. 449.

Usher (1987), 'Community Finance' in *Thirty Years of EEC Law*, p. 195.

Usher (1988), 'Financial Services in EEC Law', *ICLQ*, **144**.

Van Bael, I. and Bellis, J.F. (1989), '*Competition Law of the EEC*' (2nd edn), Oxford: CCH Editions Ltd.

Vasseur, M., 'Liberté d'établissement et libre prestation des services en matière bancaire, boursière et financière dans les pays de la CEE', *Rev. Trim. Dr. Europ.*, pp. 129–39.

Vasseur, M. (1988), 'Les problems juridiques de l'Europe Financière' in *La Revue Banque* (486), pp. 40–6.

Villaert, L. (1967), 'Le droit d'établissement des banques et des autres établissements financiers', *Rev. MC* (105), pp. 469–70.

Vogelaar, W. (1975), 'The Approximation on the Laws of Member States under the Treaty of Rome', *CML Reviews*, pp. 220–8.

Wallace, H., Wallace, W. and Wedd, C. (eds) (1977), *Policy-Making in the European Communities*, London: John Wiley.

Wallace, H., Wallace, W. and Wedd, C. (1983), 'Negotiation, Conflict and Compromise: the Elusive Pursuit of Common Policies in *Policy-making in the European Community* (2nd edn), London: John Wiley.

Young (1987), 'A Free Market for Banking', Economic Intelligence Unit, *European Trends*, April.

Ypersele, J. Van and Koeune, J.C. (1985), *The European Monetary System*, Cambridge: Woodhead-Faulkner.

Zavvos, G. (1988), 'Towards a European Banking Act', *CML Review*, **25** (263) pp. 268–70.

Zavvos, G. (1988), 'The EEC Banking Policy for 1992' in *Revue de la Banque*, Brussels (3), March–April, pp. 7–20.

Zavvos, G. (1988), '1992, One Market', *International Financial Law Review*, **7**, March.

Zis, G. (1984), 'The European Monetary System 1979–1984: An Assessment', *Journal of Common Market Studies*, **23** (1), September.

Index